AyDavie

Colorado Springs
Oct 1988

Riding the Waves of Change

Gareth Morgan

Riding the Waves of Change

Developing Managerial Competencies for a Turbulent World

 Jossey-Bass Publishers

San Francisco • London • 1988

RIDING THE WAVES OF CHANGE
Developing Managerial Competencies for a Turbulent World
by Gareth Morgan

Copyright © 1988 by: Jossey-Bass Inc., Publishers
350 Sansome Street
San Francisco, California 94104
&
Jossey-Bass Limited
28 Banner Street
London EC1Y 8QE

Library of Congress Cataloging-in-Publication Data

Morgan, Gareth.
   Riding the waves of change.

   (The Jossey-Bass management series)
   Bibliography: p. 201.
   Includes index.
   1. Management. 2. Organizational behavior.
3. Organizational change. I. Title. II. Series.
HD31.M6283   1988   658.4'06   87-46337
ISBN 1-55542-093-1 (alk. paper)

Manufactured in the United States of America

The paper in this book meets the guidelines for
permanence and durability of the Committee on
Production Guidelines for Book Longevity of the
Council on Library Resources.

JACKET DESIGN BY WILLI BAUM

FIRST EDITION

Code 8821

The Jossey-Bass Management Series

⟨⟨⟨ Contents

Preface   xi

The Author   xvii

1. Emerging Waves and Challenges: The Need
   for New Competencies and Mindsets   1

2. Reading the Environment   16

3. Managing Proactively   27

4. Sharing the Vision   46

5. Empowering Human Resources   54

6. Promoting Creativity, Learning, and Innovation   69

7. Developing Skills in Remote Management   86

8. Harnessing the Creative Power of Information
   Technologies   96

9. Managing Complexity and Ambiguity   125

10. Broadening Competencies and Reframing
     Contexts   136

11. Competence Programs for Managers and Their
     Organizations   168

     Appendix A: Designing C-PLAN Forums   185

     Appendix B: Notes on the Research Methodology   193

     References   201

     Index   209

᎒᎒᎒ Preface

How are the forces reshaping the world economy going to change
the nature of modern organizations?

What demands will these changes make on the competencies required of managers and their senior and junior staff in the
years ahead?

History shows that managerial competencies vary along
with the nature of environmental change. Different eras demand
different skills and abilities. Up until the 1960s, successful management often rested on the mastery of specific techniques. The
ability to combine technical, human, and conceptual skills to
create efficiency often provided a basis for success. During the
1970s and 1980s this has begun to change. While these skills
and abilities are still relevant, increased environmental turbulence has created an atmosphere of change and uncertainty that
calls for new abilities. Now more than ever, organizations and
their members face the dual problem of how to do the right
thing *and* how to do it well. In the process, the whole concept
of competence is changing. Whereas, in the past managerial
competence went hand in hand with the possession of specific
skills and abilities, it now seems to involve much more. Increasingly, it rests in the development of attitudes, values, and "mindsets" that allow managers to confront, understand, and deal
with a wide range of forces within and outside their organizations, as well as in the development of operational skills.

This book is called *Riding the Waves of Change* because
this image captures the nature of the new management chal-

xi

lenge. Managers and their organizations are confronting wave upon wave of change in the form of new technologies, markets, forms of competition, social relations, forms of organization and management, ideas and beliefs, and so on. Wherever one looks, one sees a new wave coming. And it is vitally important that managers accept this as a fundamental aspect of their reality, rise to the challenge, and learn to ride or moderate these waves with accomplishment. This will require an approach to management and the development of managerial competence that are proactive and future oriented, so that future challenges will be tackled with foresight and flexibility, and managers and their organizations will be able to deal with the opportunities created by change, rather than allow the waves to sweep over them.

This book explains in practical terms how the necessary competence can be developed: first, by discussing and illustrating the kinds of managerial and organizational competencies that are needed to navigate and be effective in a turbulent world. And second, by illustrating how organizations can develop competence plans (C-PLANs) that will sharpen and renew their ability to stay on the cutting edge of new developments.

Riding the Waves of Change is based on the findings of research that involved senior executives in an action-learning project designed to explore the implications of key environmental trends for the future of their organizations. These executives met in small groups in round table settings and looked for what I call *fracture lines* in the environment—those points of change and transformation that have the potential to alter the nature of whole industries, services, and their constituent organizations. The mandate was to identify significant fracture lines and then to specify the competencies that will be necessary to deal with the consequences as they unfold over time. In the chapters that follow, I have synthesized the insights that emerged from these discussions, using the executives' own words wherever possible. I have also developed the methodology used in the research project into the C-PLAN process for identifying and developing required competencies.

Thus, the book will be of interest to anyone who wishes to gain a better understanding of how to become more proactive and skilled in dealing with the managerial turbulence that lies ahead. Senior executives will find numerous ideas and frameworks through which they can think about the broader environment and begin to launch competence programs and other initiatives suited to the needs of their organizations. Human resource management, corporate planning, MIS, and other staff will find many ideas that will be useful in shaping their own contributions to future effectiveness. And middle managers will gain insight into how their future role is likely to change and how they can position themselves for these challenges. The book addresses trends and competencies that are likely to influence every sector of society. It is designed to be relevant to people working in virtually all types of organizations.

Overview of the Contents

Riding the Waves of Change contains eleven chapters and two appendixes. Chapter One presents an overview of some of the emerging waves and challenges facing organizations and describes the competencies and mindsets that will be necessary as we move toward the twenty-first century. The remaining chapters explore these competencies in greater detail.

Chapter Two examines the problem of reading environmental change; I suggest that a search for potential *fracture lines* can provide a powerful means of identifying trends and issues that may transform one's organization.

Chapter Three focuses on how one can approach change proactively—by developing opportunity-seeking mindsets, an "outside-in" approach to management, and positioning and repositioning skills.

The focus in Chapter Four is on the importance of leadership in providing an overall sense of vision and direction for an organization.

In Chapter Five, I address the importance of valuing and developing human resources and of promoting managerial styles that will empower employees to be innovative and self-organizing. This theme is further developed in Chapter Six, in which I discuss the importance of encouraging creativity, innovation, and learning.

Chapter Seven introduces the concept of "remote management" and explores problems of managing in flat, decentralized organizations. It gives special attention to the ideas of "helicoptering," "managing through an umbilical cord," and making support staff more client oriented.

In Chapter Eight, I explore how information technology can be used as a truly creative force to refine products and services and to help create the flatter organization structures and decentralized styles of management discussed in Chapter Seven. Problems relating to the planning and use of the new technology are also explored, along with issues relating to the management of information and the development of software.

Chapter Nine focuses on the problems of managing in an environment of complexity and change, especially when paradoxical demands are imposed by competing stakeholders and multiple performance requirements.

In Chapter Ten, I address the problem of broadening competence to embrace and influence relations outside one's organization. This chapter confronts the fact that some of the most important problems facing modern organizations are rooted in the broader socioeconomic contexts in which they operate: for example, in patterns of global competition, levels of economic growth, patterns of government regulation, the industrial relations climate, social attitudes, and the quality of political leadership at national and local levels. Chapter Ten explores how organizations can begin to reshape these problems through developing "contextual competencies" that focus on bridge building between different sectors of society, reframing shared problems to create new solutions, blending the ability to act locally and nationally, and developing a new sense of social responsibility.

Chapter Eleven—which is supplemented by a resource item in Appendix A—focuses on competence development generally. In this chapter, I emphasize the importance of building a "competence mindset" into everything one does and developing in-house competence development programs that generate an ongoing capacity for innovation and renewal. The C-PLAN provides step-by-step guidance on how this can be done. I also suggest in this chapter that management education programs can give more prominence to the managerial competencies and learning processes discussed in this book. In this way, the book specifies some of the competencies that managers and their organizations will need in order to meet the challenges of a turbulent world, *and* it shows ways of bringing those competencies into being.

Appendix B presents a note on the methodology I used in the research for this volume.

Acknowledgments

Thanks are due to many people.

The research on which this book is based was funded by Shell Canada as part of York University's Emerging Managerial Competencies Project. The project was administered by a joint advisory committee composed of members of the university's faculty of administrative studies—Rein Peterson (committee chairman), Alan Hockin (dean of the faculty), and William Menzel (executive in residence)—with Robert Taylor and Douglas Wade representing Shell Canada. I am grateful for all their help in launching the research and for their flow of ideas and encouragement.

My research involved contacts and discussions with dozens of senior executives, twenty of whom participated in the round table forums in which much of the research was conducted. The thoughts and ideas of these executives lie at the heart of the material presented in this volume, and I wish to thank them all.

The research project was designed and implemented with the help of Wayne Tebb, who acted as special consultant. His energy and ideas shaped the work at every stage, and I am truly grateful to have had such an excellent partner.

Finally, I wish to thank Todd Jick, Rein Peterson, Lin Ward, and Glen Taylor for their bibliographical and research contributions, and Betty Hagopian for her help in producing the final manuscript.

Toronto   Gareth Morgan
March 1988

For Karen

ᕫᕫᕫ The Author

Gareth Morgan has spent the last fifteen years studying and writing about organizations, management, accounting, corporate strategy, social philosophy, and other issues. A professor of administrative studies at York University, Toronto, he has published many books and articles, including *Images of Organization* (1986). In 1987 he was elected a fellow of the International Academy of Management in recognition of an outstanding international contribution to the science and art of management.

Morgan has held positions at a number of universities in Europe and North America and has served on the editorial boards of several journals in the field of management and organization studies. He received his B.S. degree (1965) in economics from the London School of Economics and Political Science, his M.A. degree (1970) in public administration from the University of Texas, Austin, and his Ph.D. degree (1980) in organization theory from the University of Lancaster, England.

Over the last few years Morgan has concentrated on developing and disseminating the practical implications of his research. He continues to conduct workshops on his approach to organization and management and has recently launched a new venture called "Imaginization: Directions for the Future," which focuses on developing creative approaches to organizational learning, change, and development, and on developing the competencies discussed in this book.

Born in Wales, Morgan now lives in Toronto with his wife, Karen, and their two young children, Evan and Heather.

Riding the Waves
of Change

In developing managerial competencies we must do more than "drive through the rearview mirror." It is not enough to look at what excellent organizations and managers are already doing. It is also necessary to be proactive in relation to the future: to anticipate some of the changes that are likely to occur and to position organizations and their members to address these new challenges effectively.

1

Emerging Waves and Challenges:
The Need for New Competencies
and Mindsets

Imagine a long, open Hawaiian beach. The surf is rolling in, and the waves are speckled with surfers and surfboards. Some surfers are riding the waves with flowing determination. Others are flying high into the air and plunging deep into the foam. The image provides a metaphor for management in turbulent times. For like surfers, managers and their organizations have to ride on a sea of change that can twist and turn with all the power of the ocean.

We live in times of change. And the complexity of this change is as likely to increase as to decrease in the years ahead. Numerous technological, social, and information revolutions are combining to create a degree of flux that often challenges the fundamental assumptions on which organizations and their managers have learned to operate. Managers of the future will have to ride this turbulence with increasing skill, and many important competencies will be required.

These competencies are the focus of this book, which draws on the results of an action-learning project designed to investigate the impact of changes in the world economy on the future of organization and management.

In the spring of 1986 three groups of leading Canadian executives met to take a future-oriented look at the skills and competencies that will be needed in their organizations using a special methodology. (See Appendix B for details.) They had to

identify the critical "fracture lines" likely to influence and reshape their organizations, and the mindsets, skills, and abilities
that would be required of managers in the future.

Discussions ranged widely and examined such issues as
the impact of robotics and computerization, the demand for
more creativity and innovation, the need to create market-driven
organizations, the challenge of free trade and global competition, the relationship between unemployment and lost markets,
problems with business–government relations, and the potential
for a growing polarization in society.

These discussions generated a wealth of insight into the
problems and challenges facing modern organizations and the
constructive actions that can be taken to meet them. In summary, it was felt that our organizations and their managers will
have to do much to sharpen their abilities to cope with the demands of a rapidly changing world. In addition, they will have
to find ways of moderating the turbulence of that world.

Discussions about sharpening abilities to cope generated
numerous ideas relating to the management and design of organizations in times of change, which are presented in detail in
chapters Two to Nine. Discussions relating to the problem of
moderating turbulence point toward the development of important "contextual competencies" requiring coordinated attention
from various sectors of society. These are discussed in Chapter
Ten.

In the remainder of this chapter I summarize the key insights and conclusions that emerged in these discussions by
sketching scenarios for the future, with implications for future
managerial competencies. Figure 1 gives an overview of the issues
that lie at the center of attention.

Scenario: An increasingly turbulent environment.

The pace and complexity of change are as likely to increase
as to decrease in the years ahead. Few, if any, organizations can
be sure of a secure future, as scientific and technological developments can transform the very ground on which they have
learned to operate. Changes can come from "out of the blue."
Traditional competencies or market niches can be challenged by
new technologies, generating new skills and new products. Slum-

Figure 1. An Overview of Some Emerging Managerial Competencies.

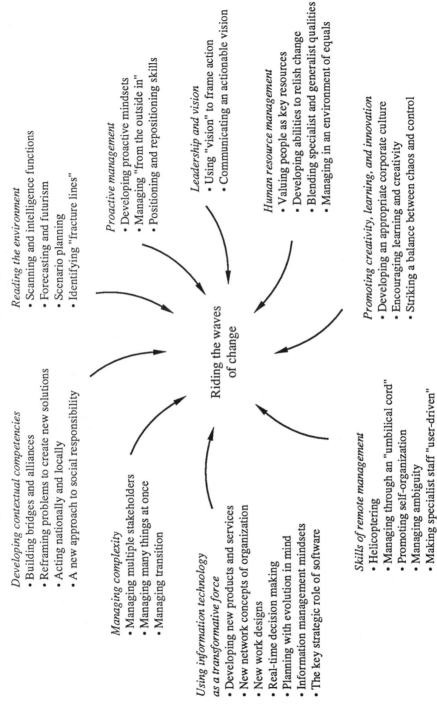

Developing contextual competencies
- Building bridges and alliances
- Reframing problems to create new solutions
- Acting nationally and locally
- A new approach to social responsibility

Reading the environment
- Scanning and intelligence functions
- Forecasting and futurism
- Scenario planning
- Identifying "fracture lines"

Proactive management
- Developing proactive mindsets
- Managing "from the outside in"
- Positioning and repositioning skills

Leadership and vision
- Using "vision" to frame action
- Communicating an actionable vision

Human resource management
- Valuing people as key resources
- Developing abilities to relish change
- Blending specialist and generalist qualities
- Managing in an environment of equals

Promoting creativity, learning, and innovation
- Developing an appropriate corporate culture
- Encouraging learning and creativity
- Striking a balance between chaos and control

Managing complexity
- Managing multiple stakeholders
- Managing many things at once
- Managing transition

Using information technology as a transformative force
- Developing new products and services
- New network concepts of organization
- New work designs
- Real-time decision making
- Planning with evolution in mind
- Information management mindsets
- The key strategic role of software

Skills of remote management
- Helicoptering
- Managing through an "umbilical cord"
- Promoting self-organization
- Managing ambiguity
- Making specialist staff "user-driven"

Riding the waves of change

bering giants can be shaken to life and left staring at new competitors, who have new ideas and new approaches and will carry developments into new realms. More than ever, the world is in flux. And organizations and their managers must recognize the necessity of developing the mindsets, skills, and abilities that will allow them to cope with this flux.

Managers of the future will have to develop their ability to "read" and anticipate environmental trends. They will need to develop antennae that help them to sense the critical issues and identify the emerging "fractures" that will transform their organizations. At present these skills are largely intuitive and the preserve of exceptionally astute individuals who have a "good nose" for new developments. One important challenge will be to find ways of developing these skills more explicitly.

Scenario: Increasing turbulence and change will require organizations and their managers to adopt a much more proactive and entrepreneurial relationship with the environment, to anticipate and manage emergent problems, and to create new initiatives and new directions for development. This proactive philosophy will be essential for empowering and energizing organizations to keep abreast of the challenges they face and will need to be dispersed throughout an organization. It will be particularly important at senior levels, especially in relation to the generation and implementation of corporate strategy.

Managers of the future will have to develop the attitudes and skills that facilitate proactive management, in particular, "proactive mindsets," an ability to manage "from the outside in," and positioning and repositioning skills that allow the pursuit of new opportunities.

Proactive mindsets are necessary if people are to approach challenges actively rather than passively. Many organizations and their managers drive toward the future while looking through the rearview mirror. They manage in relation to events that have already occurred, rather than anticipate and confront the challenges of the future. A proactive approach requires managers

- To "look ahead"
- To identify problems and opportunities

- To find ways of reframing problems so that negatives become potential positives, opening new avenues for development
- To grasp, shape, and develop these opportunities so that they can be implemented

This approach requires a "we can make it happen" philosophy that empowers people to envisage and realize desirable futures, rather than wait for the future to unfold.

Outside-in management keeps an organization in close contact with its evolving environment and enhances its capacity to rise to challenges and opportunities in an ongoing way. This outside-in philosophy contrasts with the "inside-out" philosophy so common today, where managers relate to the environment in terms of what they and their colleagues *want* to do, rather than what is necessary to meet the challenge of new technologies and the evolving demands of external stakeholders, especially customers and potential customers.

An outside-in philosophy can be developed:

- By focusing on potential transformations in production technologies and in the market to provide early warning signs of the transformations that will be required in one's organization
- By assessing the appropriateness of current strengths and distinctive competencies and transforming them when necessary
- By seeing the strengths and weaknesses of one's organization through the eyes of key external stakeholders, with the aim of strengthening and developing key competencies

Positioning and repositioning skills allow an organization to adjust to new opportunities. A number of these skills are likely to become increasingly important, including

- An ability to manage tensions between present and future, so that one can position for the future while avoiding collapse in existing operations. This ability is particularly important in achieving major strategic transformations, and requires the development of managerial attitudes and structures that aid rather than hinder transition.

- An ability to develop "change experiments" that can test the feasibility of different lines of development and thus create a range of opportunities for large-scale change through an incremental "trial-and-success" approach that does not place the entire organization at risk.
- An ability to balance creativity and discipline, so that imagination and flair are always backed by the disciplined effort necessary to make good ideas good realities.
- An ability to achieve "good timing" in relation to the introduction of new technologies and entry into new markets, because in times of rapid change timing often spells the difference between success and failure.

Scenario: First-rate leadership will increase in importance at all levels of organization, but it will not necessarily be highly formalized or hierarchical. Increasingly, the leadership process will become identified with an ability to mobilize the energies and commitments of people through the creation of shared values and shared understandings.

Managers of the future will have to develop their leadership skills. In particular, they will have to view leadership as a "framing" and "bridging" process that can energize and focus the efforts of employees in ways that resonate with the challenges and demands posed by the wider environment. This process requires many competencies, especially those that enable the leader to create or find the vision, shared understanding, or sense of identity that can unite people in pursuit of relevant challenges; and to find means of communicating that vision in a way that makes it actionable.

Managers of the future must pay special attention to skills that increase their power to communicate, to create shared understanding, to inspire, and to empower others to take on leadership roles. The leader of the future will not always lead from the front; in times of uncertainty, a significant part of a leader's role rests in finding ways of unlocking the ideas and energies of others. He or she must articulate a relevant sense of direction, while broadening ownership of the leadership process so that others are also encouraged to bring forward their ideas and thus influence the direction that the organization actually takes.

Scenario: In an information society the management of an organization's human resources will become increasingly important. Managers will have to find ways of developing and mobilizing the intelligence, knowledge, and creative potential of human beings at every level of organization. Traditional economics has taught us that the important factors of production are land, labor, and capital. But in the modern age, knowledge, creativity, opportunity seeking, interpersonal skills, and entrepreneurial ability are becoming equally important.

The process of human resource management will thus become an important function of every manager's job, rather than the preserve of personnel specialists. Managers will have to become increasingly skilled in placing quality people in key places and developing their full potential.

It will become increasingly important to recruit people who enjoy learning and relish change and to motivate employees to be intelligent, flexible, and adaptive. Special attention will need to be devoted to finding ways of motivating people to make contributions that have long-term benefits, not just those that become visible in the short run. New ways of balancing and integrating the interests of shareholders and employees will also have to be developed.

As organizations become more aware of the importance of their human resource base and increase the quality of their human resources, the nature of the manager's role will also change. The manager will no longer be able to function as a technical specialist who is also responsible for managing people, as is so often the case today. He or she will have to become much more of an all-round generalist who is able to achieve good integration between technical, human, operational and creative sides of management. The skill of integrating short- and long-term perspectives will become of increasing importance as a means of integrating today's learning with future activities. Every manager will be required to think of tomorrow as well as be effective today.

Increasingly, managers of the future will have to be able

to manage in an environment of equals and will have to prove their worth by being a resource to those being managed, as troubleshooters, resources, idea generators, problem solvers, team builders, networkers, orchestrators, facilitators, conflict managers, and motivators. The concept of manager will be transformed as organization structures become flatter through the removal of traditional supervisory roles.

The new managerial qualities will initiate new realms of opportunity for women in organizations because women have a much stronger record than men in developing many of these key people-management skills.

Scenario: The demands of an information society will require organizations and their members to promote creativity, learning, and innovation. They will have to find the key to unleashing individual creativity and learning, and develop organizational processes and structures that promote this.

Organizational hierarchies tend to stifle debate and risk taking. Managers interested in promoting learning and innovation thus have to find new ways of structuring relations to promote the creative process, especially through the values defining corporate culture. The ability to foster an appropriate culture will become increasingly important, especially one permeated by attitudes that encourage openness, self-questioning, a proactive entrepreneurial approach, an appreciation for the importance of "adding value," and a general optimism and orientation toward learning and change that energizes people to rise to challenges.

Managers will also need to promote innovation through brainstorming, creative thinking, and experimentation and by developing reward structures that sustain innovative activity. They will have to develop more open managerial processes that flatten hierarchies and improve lateral interactions. The ability to manage and work within multidisciplinary teams will be essential. Communications, meeting, and project-management skills will become increasingly important.

Scenario: The flattening of organization structures will require new approaches to management and control. With the props of hierarchy removed, managers will have to coordinate through the development of shared values and shared understanding and find the right balance between delegation and control.

Managers will become responsible for coordinating the work of people who want to work with a minimum of supervision. Managers will need to learn to "let go," and to develop skills of "remote management," such as "helicoptering" and "managing through an umbilical cord." Managers will have to promote decentralization and become skilled in designing and managing systems that are self-organizing.

The "hands-off" style demands a very different philosophy and approach from that required of managers working in hierarchical situations. Managers must become adept at handling the uncertainty and ambiguity that accompany remote management and at reading the early warning signs suggesting when intervention is needed. Management will become much more concerned with empowerment than with close supervision and control.

Innovation is likely to become more "line driven," and managers of specialist "service" departments, such as R&D and MIS, will have to develop more "client-oriented" approaches that tailor professional skills and standards to the requirements of users. In many cases, their departments will develop into autonomous entrepreneurial businesses serving clients outside as well as inside the parent organization.

The pace of change and the required evolution of skills will place a high premium on continuous learning. Managers will have to become finely tuned to their own learning needs and those relating to the education and development of their staff. In many cases, they will have to become exceptional educators in "on-the-job" activities.

Scenario: Information technology—in the form of microcomputing, electronic communication, and robotics—has the capacity to transform the nature and structure of many organizations and the nature and life cycles of their products and services. Organizations that fail to get "on board" and to reap the potential benefits will find the competition passing them by. The technology is leading us into a new age in which completely new styles of organization and new managerial competencies will come into their own.

Managers of the future will have to become increasingly skilled in understanding how computer-based intelligence can be

used to develop new products and services and to redesign existing ones. Products and services that are "smart," "multipurpose,"
"user driven," and capable of evolving in design point toward
the future of many industries and services. The trends are already evident in many areas of the economy; for example, in
how microcomputing has transformed products like typewriters
into word processors and banking and other financial services
into automated transactions.

The rapid pace of technological change will require important management skills, especially in relation to the management of short product life cycles with short payback periods
and in relation to the timing and scale of technological innovation and change.

The new technology can be used to reinforce bureaucratic
"top-down" styles of organization. But its true potential rests in
promoting decentralization, network styles of management, and
capacities for self-organization. The technology has a capacity
to dissolve organizational hierarchies by creating smaller-scale,
loosely coupled organizational units coordinated electronically,
where work units can remain separate yet integrated. The technology facilitates new work designs that are flexible and self-
organizing, where the network rather than the pyramid is the
primary organizational form.

The technology will also transform interorganizational relations, dissolving rigid boundaries between separate organizations and creating more open patterns of interaction. This trend
is vividly illustrated in the "Just in Time" (JIT) management
systems, which, supported by sophisticated information technology, create new connections among suppliers, subcontractors,
manufacturers, unions, retailers, and customers. Organizations
of the future are much more likely to form elements of a loosely coupled network of subcontracted relations, where boundaries are intermeshed rather than discrete.

All these changes will have important consequences for
managers of the future. Management of interorganizational relations will become as important as management of intraorganizational relations, and skills in achieving nonbureaucratic modes
of coordination, especially through development of some sense

of shared purpose and identity and through the use of first-rate communications systems, will need to be acquired. Extensive use will be made of such electronic modes of coordination as electronic mail and video conferencing and of other management information systems.

The speed of communications fostered by computer technology will exert a major impact on decision-making systems. Managers will have to cope with an increased pace of work, where key decisions must be made "on-line" in "real time." Bureaucratized systems of decision making have often created, and have been used to create, time for decision makers. Electronic communications will speed information exchange and force tighter deadlines that will not allow procrastination. "Real-time decision making" will become an important skill, and will become an important criterion for judging the effectiveness of managers in key operational roles.

The new modes of electronic communication will increase the amount of data available in decision making, creating the problem of information overload. Managers will have to learn to overcome the paralysis, or clouding of issues, that can result from having too much information and develop "information management mindsets" that allow them to sort the wheat from the chaff. Skills in the design of information systems, data management, and data analysis and interpretation will become increasingly important. Managers will also have to be more computer literate and learn to dialogue electronically—with both people and data—with a high degree of skill.

The new technology will also demand new planning mindsets, so that the development and implementation of the technology can evolve along with the advances and the learning that occur with use. The nature of the technology favors small-scale, experimental, "step-at-a-time" projects. The approach to planning must reap the benefits of this incremental, learning-oriented approach, while keeping the "bigger picture"—the need for wider modes of integration and system compatibility—clearly in mind. Rather than developing large-scale, "total systems engineering" approaches based on clear "predesigns," organizations will develop "user-driven" approaches that achieve consistency and integration of technical and data management systems, for example, through identification and management of critical parameters. This approach will place users in the driving seat, and place MIS and other technical experts in a supportive rather than directive role.

The new technology will create great opportunities for the software industry, which is in the position to link the developments in hardware to cutting-edge implementation. At present, many organizations delegate the development of cutting-edge management systems to software engineers, both those within the software industry and their own MIS department staff, in effect saying: "We want this, and we'd like you to do it for us." To achieve this task, those developing software must have a thorough understanding of the new managerial and organizational principles underlying the systems that they will be expected to design. The software industry and MIS departments will have to recruit some of the best managerial minds, and people skilled in the new approaches to organizational design. Effectiveness here will be a critical factor influencing the future competence of management in general.

Scenario: Complexity is the name of the managerial game: many managers may want simplicity, but the reality is that they have to deal with complexity. The complexity of organizational life is increasing rather than decreasing, as manifested in the conflicting demands posed by multiple stakeholders, the need for managers to deal with many things at once, and the almost continuous state of transition in which organizations exist.

To manage ambiguity and paradox, managers of the future will have to develop managerial philosophies and techniques that allow them to cope with messy, ill-defined situations that do not lend themselves to clear-cut interpretation, and have no ready-made recipes for action.

Shareholders, employees, unions, customers, collaborating firms, government agencies, the local community, and the general public will be active stakeholders in the organization, imposing their own demands on management. The situation is even more complicated for senior executives in conglomerates, where different businesses falling under the same corporate umbrella may each have a complicated set of stakeholders. Managers of the future will be faced with the "stakeholder concept of organization," as opposed to the present "shareholder concept," and will have to recognize the multiple sets of interests that must be served and reconciled. They will require many political and networking skills to blend the contradictory demands.

Managers will have to be adept at managing many things simultaneously. They will have to combine specialist and generalist skills and learn to achieve excellent performance in many areas simultaneously. They will have to find ways of reframing contradictory situations so that new opportunities and problem solutions become apparent. And they will have to recognize that any situation typically has multiple meanings (to different stakeholders) that have to be managed or integrated in some way.

Managers of the future will also have to become increasingly skilled in managing transition. They will have to recognize flux as the norm and develop mindsets and skills that allow them to cope with the continuous flow of new ideas, products, technologies, skills, information, and interpersonal and interorganizational relations. In some cases, they will have to deal with crisis as a norm, for example, where product life cycles are so short that routine product development and production must be managed with the speed and precision typically required of emergency situations. Managers of the future will have to learn to ride these and other turbulent conditions by going with the flow, recognizing that they are always managing *processes* and that flux rather than stability defines the order of things.

Scenario: In addition to reading about and dealing with emerging trends, managers of the future, especially those at a senior level, will have to find ways of reshaping those trends so that they become more manageable. The proactive approach to management will have to embrace an ability to reshape the socioeconomic environment and not just treat it as a given.

Many of the most important problems facing our organizations are contextual, in the sense that they are rooted in the socioeconomic environment. American, British, Canadian, French, Japanese, Scandinavian, and other nationally based organizations face particular sets of problems that are vitally

linked with the national and international context in which
they are operating. For example, issues relating to a country's
competitive position in the world—such as the effects of government regulation, the climate of labor–management relations, the
"national psyche," the growing problems associated with youth,
unemployment, and unsatisfied social expectations, national
and local politics, the quality of the educational system, and the
globalization of trading relations—exert a major impact on the
performance of organizations within the country. Future managers in all nations face the challenge of influencing and reshaping these problems and relations through the development of
"contextual competencies" that mobilize action from key
actors in different sectors of society.

Skills in "bridge building," and other forms of collaborative activity uniting diverse stakeholders in attacks on shared
problems, will be at a premium. Partnerships and other joint
ventures, and new understandings between organizations in different sectors of the economy—such as business, education, government, labor, human services, and voluntary sectors—will be
needed to attack unemployment, illiteracy, skills training, pollution, and a variety of social issues. All sectors have a stake in
these problems, and novel ways of addressing them must be
found. In particular, resources will need to be rechanneled to
critical areas, and organizational activities will require new
methods of regulation that rely on the development of shared
values and understanding, rather than bureaucratic rules that
hamper effective action. New ways of combining local and national attacks on problems are also necessary to avoid the inaction that often arises when stakeholders wait for broad national
initiatives to emerge, rather than try to operate on both fronts
simultaneously.

Finally, managers of the future will have to develop a
much greater sense of social responsibility—not just for lofty
moral reasons, but because in a complex, interdependent society, a high degree of responsibility needs to be integrated into
the way managers *think about* their relationship with the wider
context. Indifference to the social implications of organizational
actions scares the public, undermines confidence, and almost al-

ways backfires, especially in the long run. A greater understanding of the importance of developing along with the wider context will lead to creative solutions to many socioeconomic problems. The interdependence of economy and society means that socially responsible action is not just a luxury. In the long term, it is a necessity. Managers of the future will recognize this and approach their activities in ways that allow their organizations to evolve along with society.

Development of these contextual competencies will require a form of corporate statesmanship that uses skills of "outside-in management" to help create the conditions through which society can flourish. These skills will help managers to shape the waves of change that they eventually ride.

In the following chapters I look more closely at these issues and discuss some concrete ways in which managers and their organizations can develop the mindsets, skills, and general competencies that will allow them to manage the challenges that lie ahead.

2

Reading the Environment

The following comments from two CEOs get to the core of the issues explored in this chapter:

> All business leaders must learn to look externally; the world is now a trading village: it's no good looking at your own problems or needs to the exclusion of all else.

> CEOs must come to grips with the seven or eight issues crucial to their organization; and that's an important skill!

As the socioeconomic world grows more turbulent, an ability to understand one's organization and position it to deal with emerging trends becomes more and more important. Few if any organizations can now feel secure in their niches. For in a world that is in a continuous state of transformation, there is no guarantee that any set of products, services, skills, technologies or markets will remain relevant. More than ever, those leading our organizations need to look externally, "read" what is happening in the world at large, and identify pivotal changes. They and their management teams must develop skills and mindsets that allow them to recognize significant trends and come to grips with their significance for the future.

This ability to anticipate and deal with the future is becoming a very important managerial competency. CEOs, in particular, must acquire this skill. They can do much in a personal capacity, for as one executive put it, good CEOs are always "tuning into the future" and "engage in perception gathering twenty-four hours a day." But there is also more that can be done: by finding ways of empowering other key members of their organizations to anticipate and help shape what is going to happen in decades to come.

The key word here is "empowering." The critical competency is that of *empowering* organizational members to be successful in dealing with what can be an overpowering task.

To illustrate, consider the map of environmental forces presented in Figure 2. This represents the complexity of the modern socioeconomic environment, illustrating the interdependence that exists among the different elements. Forty-seven trends that have an impact on modern organizations are identified, and still, the picture is far from complete. Yet even among these trends there are over two thousand potential lines of *direct* interaction. Different trends often impact each other, creating clusters of trends and interrelations. Some are tightly knit; others are more loosely coupled. Sometimes they move in complementary directions; at other times they are in conflict. The turbulence that characterizes the modern environment is the direct product of this kind of interaction.

Senior executives must be able to come to grips with the significance of these trends, but in a way that allows them to act positively. So often, attempts at analysis often end up having a paralyzing effect, because it is difficult to know where to start in dealing with relevant issues. Corporate planning teams frequently experience this problem. They find it easy to engage in analysis and discussion of the future, but then run up against the problem: "Where do we go from here?" Analysis and discussion, interesting though it may be, often ends up being overwhelming and fails to be translated into effective action.

Empowering Managers to Deal with the Future

The task of empowering managers to deal with emerging trends rests in avoiding two extremes: idle stargazing and overanalysis. Over the last decade a number of useful techniques have been developed. One technique, the Delphi method, in

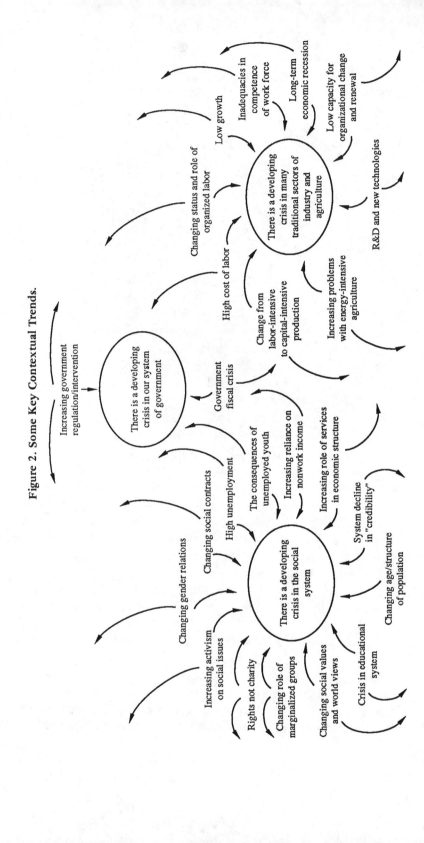

Figure 2. Some Key Contextual Trends.

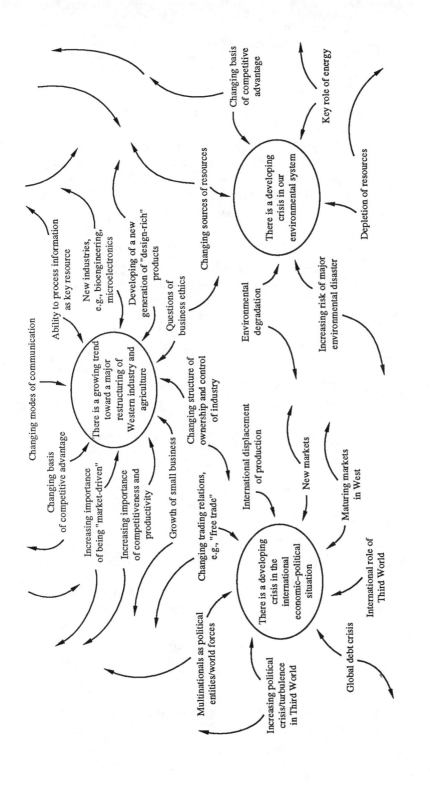

which panels of experts identify likely patterns of future development, has been incorporated into the planning process of many organizations. Numerous organizations have also established well-developed environmental intelligence and scanning functions to monitor ongoing developments and forecast changes. Others have sought the advice of futurists. And others have used "scenario planning" to sketch alternative futures, so that their organizations can plan with a knowledge of the impacts these different futures might have. These approaches will probably continue to be important in developing managerial competencies.

In addition, it is likely that techniques will be developed to zero in on particularly important changes. One characteristic of the modern socioeconomic environment is found in the frequent occurrence of forces that come together, gather momentum, and have an ability to reshape the future of entire industries or services and, hence, the nature of the constituent organizations. In my research, I have made considerable use of this idea by encouraging executives to identify and understand these emerging "fracture lines" that will define the locus for future change. This type of fracture analysis can provide the basis for important new competencies for anticipating and dealing with the future.

Looking for "Fracture Lines"

- A Bhopal or a Chernobyl
- A dramatic rise or fall in the price of oil
- A key breakthrough in some aspect of research or technology
- Radical demographic shifts
- Free trade legislation or some industry-specific decision on regulation or deregulation

Such dramatic events often signal major fractures that will seal the fate or enhance the fortune of countless organizations. Less obviously, yet equally importantly, many other changes transform the shape of social and economic relations in an ongoing fashion. Consider the following examples, which illustrate how a focus on potential "fracture lines" can be used to unravel how the future of whole industries or services may unfold.

Example 1: The Transformative Impact of "Just-in-Time" Systems of Management. Many branches of manufacturing, retailing, distribution, and other service industries are being transformed by the introduction of "Just-in-Time" (JIT) principles of management. JIT systems are an offshoot of systems designed to cut inventory and work in progress. Facilitated by the use of computers in manufacturing and stock control and by automated information systems that create on-line relations with suppliers, this approach has generated manufacturing systems in which inventory is kept to a minimum (for example, four-hour supply instead of four-day supply) and relations among suppliers, manufacturers, and retailers are closely coordinated to ensure that everything arrives immediately before it is needed. Though often seen as a technology for reducing overhead, JIT systems actually transform the management process and will probably have a major impact on the location and structure of manufacturing and related service industries.

Some of these latent consequences of JIT systems are illustrated in Figure 3. The coordination necessary for just-in-time delivery transforms relations among suppliers, manufacturers, and retailers. Formerly, a manufacturing firm may have seen itself as a separate organization. Under a JIT system, it must see itself as part of a broad interorganizational network and realize that it is this wider network of relations that must be managed. It is thus not uncommon to find manufacturers taking some responsibility for the management of their suppliers and engaging in novel methods of collaboration. Suppliers, manufacturers, and retailers increasingly have to develop new mindsets consistent with this network view of their identities.

Similarly, JIT systems transform the patterns of management and control required in an organization. Four-hour margins allow little room for error or prolonged decision making, and spread responsibility and control throughout the system. JIT systems can work effectively only if those involved are primed to spot potential problems and take corrective action. These

Figure 3. The "Fracture" Surrounding "Just-in-Time" (JIT) Management.

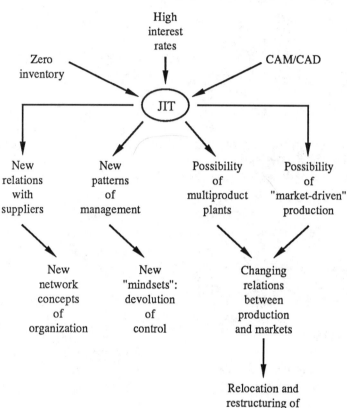

systems thus call for a new type of involvement in the work process and dissolve traditional relations between workers and managers. Every person in the system becomes a kind of manager and quality controller. Introduction of JIT systems transforms managerial hierarchies, reduces the need for middle managers, and depends for its success on the evolution of philosophies, attitudes, and mindsets that facilitate the diffusion and devolution of control. Though often introduced as a technology, it must be supported by a corporate culture that is open to these other developments. The company that uses or tries to use JIT thus invariably finds itself examining the values, beliefs, assumptions, and principles that underlie almost every aspect of its operations.

JIT systems also lend great flexibility to production systems, allowing the manufacture of different products on the same production line in almost any sequence. This flexibility is creating a potential for production plants to become "market driven" in the sense that production schedules can, in principle, be made directly responsive to the demands of retailers: customer orders can activate the system, and the product can be adapted in accordance with customers' requirements. JIT systems thus have important implications for product design and customer service and unleash possibilities for customized mass manufacture that have not previously existed. These systems also have important impacts on the economics of location and distribution. The flexibility created by JIT systems allows for the emergence of small-scale multiproduct plants located close to relevant markets, instead of the traditional large-scale single-product plants located in industrial centers. The new technology may thus end up transforming the nature of manufacturing and the location of entire industries. Extending this scenario, it does not take much to imagine how future manufacturing systems may be based on localized networks of firms held together by various subcontracting arrangements and shared management systems, geared to providing multiple products to local markets.

JIT symbolizes the unfolding effects of a "fracture line." Independent forces combine to create new management systems that have the capacity to generate further changes in the structure and identity of organizations and interorganizational relations, in patterns and philosophies of management, in corporate culture and the relations between people and their work, and in the scale, pattern, and location of industry. By tracing these consequences, many of which have yet to unfold, it is possible to glimpse what the future may have in store.

Example 2: The Transformative Consequences of Chemical-Intensive Agriculture. Social concern over toxic pollution of the environment is growing. Large-scale mechanized agriculture, which consumes as much as 20% of the output of the chemical

Figure 4. The "Fracture" Surrounding Chemical-Intensive Agriculture.

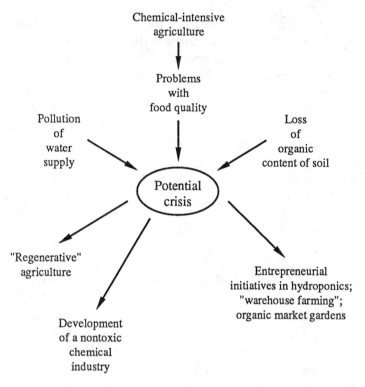

industry in North America, is a prime source and a potential fracture point in future development (Figure 4). The heavy use of chemicals is eroding the soil's organic content and hence its reproductive value (a form of capital depreciation). "Runoff" from agricultural lands is a prime contributor to the pollution of groundwater. Fungicides, herbicides, pesticides, and other toxic chemicals damage the quality of the end product (a form of food pollution). These three issues highlight related dimensions of a growing crisis.

The "crisis" is simultaneously a problem and an opportunity, because in addition to reflecting pathologies in current lines of development, it points toward paths of transformation, some of which are already beginning to unfold.

First, alternative agricultural practices (organic farming

and regenerative agriculture) are growing in importance. These practices are more in harmony with the environment and, from a marketing standpoint, can produce a better-quality product.

Second, new entrepreneurial activities capable of changing the scale and nature of agriculture are emerging (for example, through use of new technologies based on bioengineering, hydroponics, and warehouse and urban farming). Like JIT systems of management, these developments are moving the production of goods closer to the customer, thus widening the scope of further changes in the nature and structure of the food industry. In the future we are likely to see new forms of high-tech agriculture that are located in urban rather than rural areas and that supply a significant part of a community's nutritional needs.

Third, for those within and outside the chemical industry, the problems caused by toxic chemicals are creating the basis for a new direction, toward a minimally toxic future.

These three lines of opportunity, among others, signify potential lines of development of great relevance to existing firms in chemicals, agriculture, bioengineering, food production, and retailing and to the growing entrepreneurial sectors of the modern economy. By tracing potential lines of development, it is possible to anticipate important structural changes in these industries and their constituent organizations and to identify the competencies required to meet the demands that lie ahead.

Identifying Paths of Opportunity

As a number of executives involved in my research project have observed, farsighted managers always look for or try to create the fracture points that will impact their industry, because they recognize that these points define paths of future opportunity. For example, as two CEOs expressed the situation:

> Astute managers are responsible for creation
> . . . they look for fracture points . . . they recognize
> that opportunity comes with change, and that
> change creates the opportunity to do the right

things . . . . There must be a way of sensitizing people to breakpoints, and of showing them how to
handle them.

I think a healthy corporation is looking for
breakpoints, because every one of them can make a
lot of money . . . . It is a question of what is going
to happen and what *can* happen, and of being proactive in relation to that.

Fracture analysis can provide a powerful, practical tool,
which will help senior executives zero in on these fracture lines
(also called "discontinuities," "breakpoints," "sheers," and "rival scenarios") that will shape the future of their organizations.

By looking for fractures or trying to create fractures that
will have a broad, positive impact on the environment, executives will be able to combine a broad understanding of the environment with an actionable external focus. They will have a
means of identifying those issues that are crucial to the future
of their organizations. The very attempt to identify these fractures can itself make an enormous contribution, because it
sharpens the intuitive skills of entrepreneurs and strategic thinkers and broadens accessibility to these skills.

As the examples of JIT management and toxic agriculture
illustrate, many fractures unfold over time in a way that allows
us to see elements of the future *now*. Developing the anticipa-
tory aspect of management can thus be invaluable in identifying key strategic issues and keeping an organization "in sync"
with emerging waves and challenges. In Chapter Eleven, I suggest how fracture analysis can be used in a variety of settings to
stimulate and guide discussion at senior executive forums within an organization, at CEO and other forums involving members of different organizations, in "stakeholder groups," and as
the basis for task forces investigating specific areas of an organization's operations. In each case fracture analysis can do much
to help an organization read and gain a better understanding of
the external environment and position itself for what is in store.

3

Managing Proactively

> Let's face it . . . most people, when they look
> at something, tend to see the obstacles. The trick is
> to turn around and say, "What is actionable about
> this? What is the opportunity in this? How can we
> *make* an opportunity out of it?" A small percentage
> of the population will look at any important matter,
> however negative, and see the opportunity in it.
> . . . That's what we've got to encourage.

ᏋᏋᏋ Turbulence and change in the socioeconomic
environment create both problems and opportunities. To be
successful, organizations and their managers must deal with these
in a positive, opportunity-seeking way. As the CEO quoted
above suggests, this approach depends on an ability to see the
positive lines of development, however negative the situation
might seem. I will explore this proactive, entrepreneurial approach to management in this chapter in terms of three inter-
related themes: the development of *proactive mindsets*, the ability to *manage from the outside in*, and the development of
positioning and repositioning skills. Together, they provide the
profile of an emergent style of management that is sure to grow
in prominence in the years ahead.

Developing Proactive Mindsets

To what extent are our organizations still
operating in a catch-up mode, downsizing in re-

sponse to yesterday's challenge, without really coming up with tomorrow's response? . . . Many organizations are talking tomorrow, but operating in
catch-up mode. . . . How do we separate catch-up
from leap ahead, and jump on the latter?

As this quotation suggests, many organizations approach
the future while remaining locked in the past. They try to adapt
to changes that have already happened and overlook that by the
time these adjustments are made, the future has moved on. To
ride the waves of change impacting one's organization one must
do more than react. One must anticipate change and position
oneself to deal with opportunities and challenges so that one
can ride at the crest of new developments. This ability is very
much a matter of mindset. It depends on how one structures
and sees the situations one is trying to manage. Certain mindsets
can lead one into blind alleys blocked by problems, while others
can lead to situations where one can springboard from opportunity to opportunity. The executives involved in my research
project highlighted four aspects of the proactive mindset needed
for this kind of competence, which are captured here in the following phrases: "look ahead" and "drive in forward mode,"
adopt an opportunity-seeking attitude, turn negatives into positives, and be a leader rather than a follower.

Driving in "Forward Mode"

The ability to get out of a "react mode" so that one is
"in the driver's seat," shaping rather than being shaped by
change, was deemed particularly important. As one CEO
expressed the problem:

We need to keep looking ahead. . . . We need to
drive in forward mode, to get out of react mode.
We need to look at the future on a regular basis. . . .
In my organization we've been in a react mode for
years—not wanting to face the realities out there.
. . . CEOs in particular require the ability to remove
the blinkers, look ahead, step outside, and consis-

tently monitor what's coming down the pipe; they require the ability to anticipate.

Operationally speaking, this means that managers must acquire the skills discussed in Chapter Two: understanding trends and potential fracture lines and translating their implications into action plans before their effects take the organization by surprise. In particular, executives must adopt a "change can come from anywhere" philosophy and understand the context in which they are operating as broadly and deeply as possible. Executives must bring the implications of possible fractures into the present, so that they can act on appropriate issues with the future firmly in mind. Driving in forward mode means looking through the windshield rather than through the rearview mirror—watching, anticipating, and being ready to act whenever one picks up significant indications that changes may be needed now or a little way down the road.

"Opportunity Seeking"

We need to invent more opportunities and to enlarge our horizons. . . . Increasingly, we need people who can perceive opportunities, and not just come up with new ideas. It's a kind of entrepreneurship. . . . With a proactive mindset you identify opportunities in a very active way. You don't just gather information on what's there: you *create!* . . . Everyone from the CEO down needs to find ways of enlarging opportunities. . . . If we don't, then our competitors are going to put us out of business. . . . We are facing broad challenges, and we need to search for opportunities on a macro basis. . . . We will need to develop this skill in the future. In the past we've been concerned mainly with optimizing the use of scarce resources, never much more. Now we have to go beyond [this kind of] stewardship. In the new environment we have to invent demand [for products and services], and new skills and attitudes are necessary.

Whenever the executives involved in my research talked about the problems of their organizations or the challenges of the environment, the idea that opportunity seeking must be promoted as a fundamental aspect of management invariably arose. Though often seen as a function of personality and experience, opportunity seeking can be institutionalized as a corporate value by encouraging people to develop an optimistic "there must be a way of dealing with this" approach to everything they do. More often than not, employees are just asked to discharge the functions and duties associated with their role in an organization. They are rarely asked to identify and develop new opportunities as well. Yet this is precisely the kind of orientation that can invigorate and empower people to reach the leading edge of change *and* stay there.

Turning Negatives into Positives

Negative aspects of situations can be used as reference points for creating new opportunities. A number of CEOs expressed this sentiment in the following terms:

You have to turn the negatives into positives.

Competitive forces force *me* to become more competitive.

Sometimes, from those dark holes, you tend to look and say "What's available?" and you start to produce.

By identifying all the negatives out there you can identify really nice, profitable opportunities. But you have to list them; you have to identify them and look around. Discussing those negatives is now part of our [corporate] culture. We call them major factors, but they always tend to be negative. We identify them, get them on the table, and ask "How are we going to drive a strategy around them?"

This approach is well illustrated in the philosophy of an organization that has extensive relations with government and other public organizations and has to deal with a tangle of regulations and interest groups to secure contracts. Rather than fight the regulations and differing viewpoints, managers view them as constraints that must be tackled in a creative way. Their approach is to identify all the negative factors relating to the project as early as possible (for example, those likely to add to costs or create delays) and then forge a creative design that either eliminates the basic problems or meets them in a direct and satisfactory manner. The potential problems result in special features that help to sell the project and make it a success.

The approach is also captured in the philosophy of the CEO who remarked:

> If there is a highly stable market area in my industry, then I will take a close look and try to create some change. We create change to keep at the front edge!

Turning negatives into positives provides a powerful means of identifying critical areas for improving or transforming products, services, technologies, delivery systems, and other aspects of one's enterprise. It also helps to define the specific parameters around which improvements can be built. As one of the CEOs quoted above suggests, if you can get the negatives on the table you can discuss and examine them and then begin to build innovative solutions around them. The identified problems serve as springboards for arriving at new designs.

Leading Rather than Following

> You have to be ready to move very quickly. ... If you can get to the point where you are ahead, and everybody else reacts to you, and keep that rolling, you will be very successful.

> The difference between us and one of our competitors (which has moved from a $70 million

profit to a $10 million loss in only two years) is
the difference between who was first and who was
second. The difference, the largest variable, and
our research shows it, was innovation. . . . We were
first in terms of changes across the board.

Being number one, whether in implementing
a production process or recognizing a trend, is
where the action is these days—recognizing things
ahead of other people, being aware of what is coming down. We sometimes get hung up on words and
phrases out of books and studies, but the fact is: if
there is something out there that is going to happen, you had better recognize it, and you had better be doing the things now which will help you
through that situation.

These comments reinforce a point made earlier: it is
usually much better to introduce initiatives than respond to
those of others. The essence of the proactive mindset rests in
this positive, energetic approach to the management of internal and external relations. Recognizing that in a changing world
the choice is that of changing or being changed, the person with
the proactive mindset favors action rather than reaction. Sometimes this means "going with the flow" of anticipated events; at
other times it means trying to alter the nature and direction of
the flow, especially through interaction with other key players.
As will be apparent after reading Chapter Ten on the development of "contextual competencies," proactive management
may lead to various joint ventures related to shared concerns
that can transform the environment in very significant ways.

Managing from the "Outside in"

A proactive relationship with the environment implies that
close contact with that environment is important; however,
there is a vast difference in doing this from the "inside out" as
opposed to the "outside in."

Many organizations are preoccupied with inside-out management. They approach, understand, and act in relation to their environment in terms that make sense from *internal* divisions and perspectives or in terms of what powerful members *want* to do. As a result, they often act in fragmented and inappropriate ways.

Other organizations try to build from the "outside in"— they "embrace" the environment holistically and shape internal structures and processes with this wider picture in mind. They use the views and needs of customers and other key stakeholders as a mirror in which they see and understand their own strengths and weaknesses, and they act on these insights to reshape their relations with the environment. This outside-in approach to management is the focus of an important managerial competency that can be developed in various ways. The executives involved in my research identified three specific means of promoting this approach: really understanding one's market; choosing appropriate frontiers for development; and trying to see one's organization through the eyes of external stakeholders, especially competitors.

Understanding One's Market: Understanding Oneself

When managers talk about sustaining a market orientation they usually mean "doing good market research," "listening to customers," and "trying to find rewarding niches." However, there is another approach: one that treats the marketplace as a domain that can change dramatically in a way that may require redefinition and transformation of the firms that serve that domain. From this perspective, one's market and the potential transformations of that market can be used as a kind of mirror to see oneself now and in the future.

This perspective lends a new and deeper quality to the idea of sustaining a market orientation, because it emphasizes that in times of rapid change the ability to keep in touch with a market often hinges on a question of self-identity. To illustrate, consider the following example provided by an executive involved in my research:

I'm the director of a small printing company,
and we print a lot of bank checks. Well, what is technology going to do? Is there going to be a market
for bank checks? We who use checks can't tell. [To
find out] we have to go to the technology guys
and say, "Ten years down the road, how are people
going to be making payments? Are they going to
be using little pieces of paper, using plastic debit
cards, or what? And if [the latter] is the defining
market, how do we handle that? Will the market
for printed checks disappear completely, or will
there be some sort of residual?" My company must
be market driven, but the present purchasers of the
product can't tell you what the market is going to
be like. They don't know. It's the technology boys
in town who know.

The printing firm is faced with a dilemma: How does it
stay in business? Should it secure a niche that keeps it in the
paper printing trade, or should it move in new directions that
involve new technologies, perhaps outside the printing trade?

This dilemma is shared by many other firms in a wide
variety of fields. For example, many financial service firms have
had to rethink their products and identities. Such traditionally
separate services as banking, consumer credit brokerages, real
estate, and insurance have become integrated in "one-stop" financial centers. These services are now being built from a *customer standpoint,* rather than from a *production* or *supplier
standpoint,* thus requiring the suppliers to rethink what they are
all about. And the trend is widespread. For example, many consumer goods manufacturers are moving to a customer- rather
than production-oriented view of their products—integrated
stereo, TV and other audiovisual systems, rather than separate
televisions, radios, record players, telephones, and computers.

In times of rapid change, the whole idea of sustaining a
market orientation thus assumes a new dimension. As the examples indicate, it often requires organizations to step outside traditional frames of reference and see themselves from a new per-

spective. This involves more than market research and talking with one's customers (though these are very important activities). It involves monitoring a wide range of trends and developments that can signal emerging possibilities, as well as doing one's utmost to make possibilities happen. The marketing function becomes fused with planning and R&D and becomes integral to the processes through which managers understand the raison d'être of their organization and how it is likely to evolve. In approaching its market in this way, an organization can truly get outside itself and the mindsets and biases it normally takes for granted and begin to decide what it can and should be with an external rather than internal viewpoint.

Choosing Frontiers for Development

An outside-in perspective leads managers to ask fundamental questions about their organizations and, in the process, to address key choices regarding frontiers for future development.

What business are we really in?
Are we a product?
Are we a technology?
Are we a distribution system?
Are we just a "market niche"?

As is well known, such questions do much to help organizations understand their distinctive character and competencies and how these can be changed to advantage. As one executive put it:

If we see ourselves as being defined by the tasks we are performing right now, we may be less able to see what else we could be doing. Our product influences our description of ourselves.

This same executive went on to say that many of the important breakthroughs for a company rest in changing focus and pursuing new lines of development. For example:

Typically, integrated oil companies are providers of oil products to the consumer, but you see the shrewd ones becoming more like traders of products. They have changed their emphasis to that of a trading company. There are other industries that are moving in the same direction. For example, there are organizations that are shifting out of manufacturing into the business of providing products to consumers [by putting their label on products produced by others]. That is their job. And that restructures the nature of their business.

Here are some other examples of how the executives involved in my research pursued the question of corporate identity and its influence on the definition and selection of possible frontiers for development:

Are we an insurance company or in the financial services industry? Are we going to specialize in selling a range of separate financial packages or in selling investment services concerned with financial planning?

Are we a printing firm producing bank checks, or a firm meeting the evolving requirements relating to the documentation of financial transactions? Are we in the paper printing trade? Or are we a firm that seeks to operate with a variety of technologies?

Are we in the motorcycle business or in the distribution of leisure products?

Are we an integrated oil company moving resources from the ground to a consumer, or are we a commodity trading company?

Are we in mining or refining?

Are we a producer of electronics hardware or in the information-management business?

We are manufacturers; should we be distributors who subcontract the manufacturing?

We're in metal stamping; should we be in plastics?

We're a software firm; as more and more programming is built onto silicon chips should we become a troubleshooting firm that specializes in making computer systems work in practice?

These executives also emphasized the importance of being clear about the different functional capacities and strengths on which one's organization relies for future expansion, for example:

- Innovation
- Product differentiation
- Marketing and promotional skills
- "Service" and continuing customer relations
- Low-cost production
- Distribution
- Development of collaborative relations with other actors

A great deal of time was spent by the executives involved in my research in contemplating the importance of these bases for competitive advantage, and how they can be combined, as no one factor usually provides a sure recipe for success. Here are some examples of how these executives thought the issue of competitive advantage applied in their organizations:

I believe that the success of my organization [in the packaged goods industry] has more to do with our laboratory engineering people than with the $50 million we spend on advertising. . . . The marketing efforts [of different organizations] neutralize each other. . . . You have to have it, but the market is more sensitive to innovations in your product.

[In my industry—electronics] you need good marketing and a fast production line, because you need to get the product out of the door before the competitors come.

In my industry [electronics/communications] we recognize that an organization can't distinguish itself in the marketplace significantly through product advantage or technological advantages. These are very short term. They last a matter of months, and then the competition is there. [So you have to] be distinguished by response to customer needs.

A focus on adding value at every stage [in software development] would set us apart from our competitors.

If you're a low-cost producer you can always serve your customer. If you're a high-cost producer you have less room to maneuver. Quality is not enough. For example, successful quality producers like IBM force the price down and the competition out. If you can make money in bad times, you'll be OK in the good. In inflationary times you can pass on your sins of omission; in deflationary times you can't—it's too competitive.

We are under attack [by new companies entering the automotive parts market] so we are trying to go with distribution strength. My management team knows that we have to become more market driven; we have to control more distribution; we have to expand our product range, to make us more important to our customers. If we can get

the distribution in place we will be able to hold off
the competition.

It is unwise to generalize on which frontiers are most important. It depends on the evolving character of the situation
with which one is dealing, in terms of the structure of competition with which one is faced, the length of product life cycles,
and other factors. The important point is that managers should
approach the positioning process systematically and critically,
choosing those frontiers for development that keep them in close
touch with the demands of the changing environment.

Understanding Oneself Through the Eyes of Key Stakeholders

An outside-in approach to management can also be fostered by focusing on key stakeholders in the environment. For
example, an organization can learn much about itself by asking
senior executives to define its main competitors.

Who are our competitors now?
How are they competing with us?
What does this tell us about the critical frontiers on which
   we are conducting business?
How can we change these frontiers to be more effective?
If we change, who will our new competitors be?
How can we be effective in relation to these new com-
   petitors?
Where will our competition be coming from in five years?
   In ten years? In twenty years?
What does this tell us about the frontiers on which *we*
   will have to do business?
What new competencies will we need to develop?
What transitions will we have to make?

This line of questioning can be enormously constructive.
It encourages an outside-in approach to the identification of
existing and potential frontiers for development, especially
when an organization recognizes that its main competition may

be coming from outside its immediate business domain. As one executive put it:

> When the competition seems to be coming from outside rather than from inside your industry, you need a new understanding of the business you're in.

The point has relevance for many industries and organizations: for courier firms and the Post Office confronting competition in the form of national and international electronic mail; for schools, universities, and business schools facing increasing competition from market-oriented educational programs launched in the private and corporate sectors; for Western manufacturing firms confronting the reality of competition in the Third World; for copper producers facing the challenge of fiber-optics and plastic pipes; for unions facing the problem that they can't unionize robots and microprocessors; and so on.

When one views the competition in broad terms, one finds it difficult to avoid rethinking the nature of one's business and the strategies being pursued. Further, when the specific strengths and weaknesses of one's organization are identified from the standpoint of potential competitors, many detailed operational insights relevant to the present emerge. One executive described how the planning process in his organization is energized by producing "competitor plans." Regular task forces are established with the mandate of adopting the perspective of a primary competitor and of producing a plan that gives that competitor an advantage. This view from the outside, free from the constraints of how the organization presently conducts business and free from the internal politics of decision making that lead people to favor a particular strategy, provides the basis for a critical evaluation of the organization's position and what it should do to take account of the strengths and weaknesses revealed by the competitor plan. This approach allows the organization to see and challenge itself openly and constructively through a process bounded only by the imagination and ingenuity of the task force producing the competitor plan.

There is great potential for making this kind of critical review a part of any organization's management process. By putting oneself in the shoes of any external stakeholder and looking with critical eyes, one can learn much about the nature of one's organization.

Positioning and Repositioning Skills

Perhaps the most important investment an organization can make is to ensure that it has the capacity to adjust to the fractures and other changes occurring in its environment.

If the jolts are coming with increasing rapidity, and greater impact, then . . . you've got to have a response capacity built in.

Proactive, "outside-in" management demands much in terms of an organization's "response capacities" and general ability to rise to the challenges of a changing environment. Executives involved in my research project were pretty well unanimous on the importance of developing such capacities, for all too often, it is in the implementation phase that potentially great projects flounder.

Many of the mindsets and skills required to create such capacities are discussed in chapters Five and Six; however, a number of specific problems often encountered in the positioning and repositioning processes demand special attention with respect to the development of future competencies and are discussed here.

Risk Taking and the Bottom Line

The positioning process raises a major paradox for many organizations, because there is often a tension between trying to achieve significant shifts in direction and maintaining healthy financial performance in the present. Major new projects can call for long- or short-term investments that put an enormous strain on the financial viability of an organization, fueling a financial conservatism that often blocks desirable change. The ability to handle this tension and to find creative ways of launching new investments are important new managerial competencies in the financial sphere. In addition, there are important social and cultural aspects of this tension, for the risk taking and change involved in any significant repositioning often run against widely held corporate values. The act of seeking to reposition an organization may itself open an executive to criticism. Two executives expressed the problem in the following terms.

> The process [of repositioning] contradicts a very strong value that has been found to be very, very responsible behavior in business . . . stick to your knitting and do what you do best.

> You are more easily punished for the risk that goes wrong than the risk that you didn't take, or the mistakes you didn't make.

The point is that corporate values may favor conservative actions rather than those with a degree of risk. The development of appropriate response capacities in an organization thus requires that close attention be devoted to these aspects of corporate culture.

Attention must also be focused on reconciling the demands for effective operation in the "here and now" with the demands required for effective repositioning. This can create much division in an organization. To quote one executive with a special interest in the problem:

> As I see it, you have to build a schizophrenic organization, one aspect of which deals with the here and now—because to make a profit this year, we've got to ship the goods out of the door, and we've got to satisfy the customers today—and another aspect of which is concerned with the long term, by building a structure that is competitive with the main business. Its purpose eventually—I know we don't articulate it this way—is to put the

here and now aspect out of business. And over a period of time it will do that. Now, that creates a tension in the organization that we don't know how to manage.

There is an important area for the development of managerial competence here. Whether we talk about the "schizophrenic" potential described above or the problems of overcoming technical or departmental divisions, effective repositioning demands an ability to rally the energies of employees so that they help rather than block the required changes.

"Packaging" Change

Many of the problems discussed above can be partly resolved in the way change is introduced and handled. For example, there are many ways of minimizing risk and exposure by moving incrementally. A CEO who had been wrestling with this issue in his own organization offered the following view:

> In the management of organizations we need to think in terms of packages. We need an ability to take opportunities and structure them into packages of incremental decisions, to avoid putting oneself totally at risk. We have to expand our horizons to take new opportunities without endangering everything. The approach needed is *not* a total systems engineering approach [where everything is laid out from beginning to end], but one which is much more incremental. It's more than experimenting, and real skills are needed. [Perhaps] we can develop clear ideas about packaging.
>
> When the strategists and systems designers get involved many blocks arise, because they can't see the endpoint. For example, [in a large corporation] it is often possible to get one's foot in the water by seeing whether an experiment can succeed: spending $10 million to see whether you

want to spend $500 million. But many corporate
thinkers say "what's the point, unless you can
move to the $500 million straight away?" They are
interested only in the big projects. But by spending
$5 or $10 million in a number of places you may
be able to get to the one that will require $500
million.

The idea that incremental, experimental approaches to
change can provide an effective approach to the repositioning
process surfaced in many guises throughout my research, and is
explored further in relation to the management of information
technology in Chapter Eight. In understanding the approach, it
is important to realize that adoption of this kind of incrementalism does not commit an organization to aimless trial and
error. The experimental approach can be implemented within
the context of a clear corporate mission. Indeed, one of the
most important repositioning skills required of top executives
rests in the ability to find ways of translating the organization's
grand schemes into "actionable packages" that can make a
vision a reality.

Balancing Creativity and Discipline

The repositioning process requires a creative, opportunity-
seeking approach; however, it also requires great discipline. Opportunities, once found, must be explored systematically. The
"schizophrenic" properties evident in the tensions created between present and future, discussed above, are also found in the
tensions between creativity and discipline. Many creative people
who thrive on the challenge, excitement, and openness of the
idea-generating process often shun the rigor required to make
their ideas a success. It is thus important to strike some balance,
which, for some organizations, will be found "in cycles of
searching for opportunities followed by working through their
effects . . . periods of entrepreneurship, followed by consolida-
tion, followed by more entrepreneurship."
    In other organizations, especially those in which innova-
tion is the main driving force, creativity and discipline must be

integrated in an ongoing way, and important managerial skills
are required.

The Importance of Timing

Finally there is the issue of making the right move at the
right time. The views of two executives involved in my research
point to the core of the problem:

> With product life cycles as short as eighteen
> months, and products sometimes taking years to
> develop, a product can be obsolete before it gets to
> market. Timing is crucial.

> You go through a technological change [fast
> production lines to minimize cost]. Then, a couple
> of years later you are going in reverse [slower lines
> with smarter machines that can make greater ad-
> justments to accommodate changing product de-
> signs, and hence consumer preferences]. This is one
> of the great problems in manufacturing and other
> fields. You say, "Hey, there is a direction," you go
> with it and invest for a three- or four-year return,
> and then the marketplace does a turnabout. You
> now have a problem. You are sitting there with ob-
> solete or unused equipment. I think this area is
> very critical for managers. I am faced with it right
> now. Do I travel this route or another? I have a
> $10 million proposal in front of me. And I look at
> it and say "I don't know."

An organization can read the environment appropriately
and make all the right decisions. But if the timing is incorrect
or the "windows of opportunity" are different from those
anticipated, the best laid plans can flounder. At the moment
there are no obvious recipes for improving managerial judgment on these difficult issues. But timing is obviously an issue
with which managers will have to wrestle as they rise to the
challenges of a changing environment.

4

Sharing the Vision

It is crucial that members of an organization be united through some shared understanding of the organization and its mission. This point was a clear and consistent theme in many discussions:

It's absolutely crucial to have a good understanding—call it whatever you want—of why you are in business and what you are doing. The rapidity of change makes it all the more important. I think this is what the great successful organizations have in the key places.

The world is such a changeable place that you need to have a well-articulated long-term sense of where you're going, which gives you the base, the confidence, to take on whatever adaptability issues come along without losing your sense of direction. You've got to respond to the issues of the moment without losing that long-term sense.

You need a sense of corporate purpose and an awareness that the organization has a personality that goes beyond what it is doing right now.

There must be a philosophy in action—a philosophy of where we're going and of the way we treat our customers, employees, and other people, [a philosophy that emphasizes] that we work for the organization as a whole, not for individual bosses.

46

Sustaining this overarching sense of corporate direction was seen as one of the most important tasks—and given the turbulence of the modern world, an extremely difficult task—facing senior management. For as the world grows more uncertain, it becomes difficult to find and communicate that coherent point of reference that simultaneously energizes and focuses the efforts of the wide range of actors typically found in the modern organization.

"A vision!"
"A mission!"
"A corporate philosophy!"
"A sense of identity!"
"A set of core values!"
"A symbolizing presence!"

Different executives expressed the nature of the focus in different ways, but in general agreed that corporate leaders need (1) to provide their organizations with an overarching sense of vision to help frame and direct the organization's efforts, and (2) to communicate that sense of vision in an actionable form.

Vision as a Frame for Action

There is an old adage that if you don't know where you are going, any old path will get you there. An innovation can be wonderful. But it can have absolutely nothing to do with where my firm is going. You have to have a vision of what you are opting into.

This point is crucial, especially in view of the ideas explored in the previous chapter. Proactive management can create a vibrance that allows an organization to recognize and exploit opportunities and challenges; however, this vibrance must have a reference point. Innovation and opportunity seeking cannot be ends in themselves, or they will lead to haphazard development.

The problem presents top management with a major paradox. They often need to encourage flexibility and innovation. Yet to develop in a coherent and ordered way, they need a clear sense of where they are going, which, when taken to an extreme, can stifle or constrain innovation.

It is thus no accident that so many executives chose to discuss development of a corporate vision in terms of the creation of a "sense of identity," "corporate personality," "philosophy," or "set of values." These formulations allow a degree of openness in the way a sense of the future is formulated. They create a frame within which other things can happen.

When people have a good sense of what their organization stands for and where it is going, they can determine the course and appropriateness of their behavior and judge whether a particular innovation will resonate with broader aims. Through this framing process innovation can be encouraged and actively developed, yet managed so that balance is achieved between opportunism and realism. Employees can develop an instinctive feel for what is appropriate. Or, as one executive put it, they can arrive at a situation where "You don't have to be told 'Here are the bounds.' You know! You can feel it. It's there!"

Communicating an Actionable Vision

You can't communicate enough times and in enough ways why we are going where we're going. [In our organization] we discuss [this] so much ... that we end up on the same wavelength. You can't do that with a job description.

CEOs must be able to synthesize, then simplify and sell this to others in terms that they can use. They must have the ability to see what *could* be and communicate this in an actionable manner.

It is often not enough to explain ... you also have to define specific actions that will make future issues more tangible.

It is one thing for top management to develop a sense of vision. It is quite another to communicate that vision in an actionable manner so that the vision becomes a reality. This ability is a critical managerial competency.

Many organizations attempt to formulate and communicate their view of the future through a "mission statement." These statements have an important role to play, because they can be used to communicate the importance of key values, for example, commitment "to innovation," "to quality products," or "to customer service." But, as a number of executives noted, the danger is that these statements can become "empty vessels" or rituals.

> The attempt to couch mission statements in terms suitable for general consumption often makes them ineffective within the organization. They become like motherhood.

Hence the view of many executives: Mission statements may be important, but certainly are not sufficient to "get people on the same wavelength" or let them "hear what's being said," "absorb the essence of the company's philosophy," and "know what they have to do without being told" and with "a strength of conviction and sense of common responsibility to make it happen."

The really important competency lies in the ability to get employees enthused and fully absorbed with the corporate philosophy, rather than to follow instructions in a mechanical way.

This topic is further explored in Chapter Six; however, a number of specific aspects of the leadership process were identified as particularly crucial.

The Leader as Symbol and Symbol Maker

Leaders inevitably come to represent their organizations.

> Their credibility and image are crucial. People watch and judge everything they do.

Like politicians and other public figures, their words and actions
have a far-reaching effect, of symbolic as well as practical value.
It is thus crucial that leaders ensure that their presence and actions send appropriate messages. For example, it is very difficult for staff to take innovation seriously if the CEO exudes
conservatism, even if the mission statement declares innovation
a high priority.

Leadership and Empowerment

> You have to generate an "optimism" and
> "sense of the possible." You have to be positive.

There are organizations in which a status quo "holding pattern"
philosophy may be appropriate. But most situations that require strong leadership call for some kind of transformation.
Thus, it is important that the leader communicate the possibility of this transformation and move his or her followers toward
the achievement of concrete results. Methods must be found to
nudge the organization in the right direction, without dictating
a detailed course of development and thus creating too much
dependence on the leader. Leadership that *empowers* seems to
be an important emerging competency.

Broadening the Leadership Process

Finally, there is the question of openness. How widespread
should debate about an organization's mission be? In some organizations, central figures who are able to develop and communicate a corporate philosophy that is very much their own emerge
as leaders. The leader symbolizes the organization and inspires
employees through his or her presence. Vision and direction
emanate from the top; the rest of the organization is concerned
with interpretation and implementation. This type of organization can be extremely effective, but its success usually rises and
falls with the leader. There is often a "vacuum," "succession
problem," or "lack of continuity" when the leader leaves.

In other organizations the process is more widely spread. Although the leader may be very strong and responsible for many initiatives, open debate is a corporate norm. This approach was well illustrated by a number of CEOs who described their attempts to create an atmosphere in which strategy evolves through debate and self-questioning. One CEO described his attempt to make strategic planning a process that mobilizes the inputs of line managers and creates a strong sense of shared ownership:

> [I believe in making] strategic planning a line function. There is a lot of value in this because it completes the circle of a bottom-up and top-down process where you're trying to be both reactive and proactive in relation to situations. You can get more people involved in the process. You push in the direction you're working at together without saying "Here is my vision," which is one opinion and may be wrong. The people who really know the business are the people on the line who are servicing the customer, producing the product, and so on. So I think that there is much of value in a group approach to strategic management. One of [my] tasks . . . is to get my line people involved in a process, debating and working toward a strategic direction on which we collectively agree. And *then* comes the evaluation . . . in the end you as the chief executive say "that's the plan that's approved, and these are the things we do." One of the imperatives is to involve people in the process so that "we think it's ours" rather than "I think it's mine!" This participative action that creates a direction is important.

Other CEOs described the importance of cultivating an atmosphere that encourages people to think in an open and challenging manner and to exert an ongoing influence on the direction followed by their organization:

> I think that one of the great strengths of my
> organization is that of self-questioning—it is en-
> couraged . . . and it makes us a stronger company.
> It is a dynamic, driving factor [especially when]
> you have a group of people who learn that any-
> thing can be questioned, including the basic struc-
> ture of the business.

> My style of organization is such that I want
> healthy debate. I want the [person] that has been
> with the company only a year to feel that he or she
> can go to the manager three levels up and say "We
> really are doing this wrong!"

This openness can broaden the leadership process and
greatly facilitate an organization's ability to evolve. Nevertheless,
the executives making these points were careful to emphasize
that it is important to cultivate an atmosphere where self-questioning is constructive rather than destructive. Open questioning
and criticism can provide the basis for learning and change;
however, it can also be the emotional outlet for griping and
allocation of blame. The line between the two is often fine. The
latter must be avoided at all costs.

An important distinction was also made between openness and democracy.

> [The aim is not to create] a democracy. It is
> not a question of nosecounting. It is not a question
> of [asking] "All those in favor?" [Rather], it is a
> question of [cultivating] the rigorous examination
> of [an] idea that will produce a clear vision—the
> right answer. That's not democracy . . . [it] is
> [more] analytical.

Leadership style is often very much a matter of personality rather than choice. As is well known, different leaders are
effective in different situations. The views of executives involved
in my research reflected this ambiguity, but they all converged

on the importance of understanding the leadership process in terms of the development of *shared values, shared direction, and shared responsibility* for the future of the organization. These issues are likely to be the basis on which many important managerial competencies are developed in the future.

5

Empowering Human Resources

I want to find the way to unleashing creativity and innovation—to give individuals the freedom to make a full and effective contribution to my organization.

How do you encourage people to let your organization become flexible, to face the issues, so that you can approach a competitive situation competitively? How do you do it? I think it's critical. We're facing a future where we'll see changes all the time. How do we organize our corporations to face change? How do you get that through to people? It's not just a communications exercise; it's a mindset. It's a different way of thinking. How can we address this issue?

The development of creative, innovative organizations that "go with the flow" and remain competitive in a highly competitive world was a challenge facing most of the executives involved in my research. Indeed, unleashing the power and creativity of our people and our organizations—even if this means only realizing and tapping the considerable potential already there—was regarded as one of the most pressing issues facing the modern manager. Many of our organizations have difficulty in doing their best. Although they show considerable promise, they fall short in their actions.

What can managers do to change this?

How can they make innovation the life blood of their organizations?

How can they promote an ability to learn and change on a continuous basis?

The development of proactive mindsets, outside-in management, and appropriate leadership and vision all have a role to play here; however, many more specific practices and policies are needed. This chapter discusses issues relating to human resource management: the importance of viewing people as a key resource, encouraging people to relish change, blending specialist and generalist qualities, managing in an environment of equals, and making education a continual process. Chapters Six and Seven develop this theme by discussing the management of learning and innovation and the skills required to create and manage flat, decentralized organizations.

People as a Key Resource

It all boils down to one thing: people, people, people, people, people. I don't care what country, or what organization, or what team you are in —it is the people and whether you can organize those people to achieve an end result that count.

If you have the right people in all your key sectors, and all of your people are keen, then you will *make* it happen.

You have to have people that get right to the important issues. Two organizations can agree to go through the same process and get the same consultant to help them, but the difference in effectiveness rests in the ability of those present to get into the issues that need to be discussed.

I want all my people to be excellent. In today's competitive environment that's exactly what

has to happen. Everyone has to be damn good, and
we have to make it all pull together. It's no use if
the person in marketing is damn good and the person in production is damn good if they can't talk
to each other. We, as chief executives, have to ensure that they all function together.

Popular opinion often leads us to conclude that money is
the most scarce and most valuable organizational resource. Every
organization understands the importance of money, and as
every manager knows, there is precious little one can do without it. But in most organizations, especially those that are not
in immediate financial difficulty, the truly key and scarce resource is *excellent people.* The executive who has excellent people in all the key places is probably the exception rather than
the rule. Many organizations find it relatively easy to commit a
million dollars to a particular line of development, but much
more difficult to get the right people to produce the desired
results.

The importance of the human element in an organization
is increasing along with the pace of change. Change demands innovation, and innovation demands that we unleash the creative
potential of our people. In a more stable world one could organize in a mechanistic way—establish and design one's organization, direct and control it from the top, and rely on middle
managers of fairly average ability to "fill slots" with workers
and oversee operations.

Now, much more is required. Bureaucracy is giving way
to new approaches that require people to exercise discretion,
take initiative, and assume a much greater responsibility for
their own organization and management. The need to remain
open and flexible demands creative responses from every quar-
ter, and many leading organizations recognize that human intelligence and the ability to unleash and direct that intelligence are
critical resources. Traditional economics has taught us that the
main factors of production are land, labor, and capital. However, as we move into an "information society" where the ability to create value through human enterprise grows increasingly

important, the principles of economics need to be revised to include such factors of production as knowledge, information, creativity, opportunity seeking, interpersonal skills, and entrepreneurship. Without an adequate supply and good management of these human factors, it simply is not possible for an organization to keep abreast of the changes in its environment with any degree of competence. Future managers will thus need to pay more attention to attracting the right people to their organization, developing human potential and fostering conditions that make this relevant and effective, and positioning and repositioning people so that they always contribute where they are most needed.

These competencies are not new. Indeed, personnel managers have long emphasized their importance. The challenge of the future, however, is to break free of the idea that human resource management skills can be delegated to specific individuals or departments and to make them an "on-line" aspect of every manager's role, in short, to make them an integral part of the mindset through which managers manage.

Relishing Change

How do you get people to be adaptive, and flexible . . . in a manner that they will relish and enjoy, and through that, get better results? And how do you position a group of people so that they enjoy change? Because a lot of people don't enjoy change. They enjoy knowing what the parameters are, so that they can leave at 5 P.M.

I have found that the key ingredient for competent management is somebody who loves change– not just copes with it, but *loves* it. Change is so much a part of our daily menu that you must really thrive on it, and get your kicks from it. The counterpressure, and I think that is what our organizations are struggling with to a large degree, is the great value that is being put on stability. And

that clash is one that competent management has
to cope with.

> Simplicity, clarity, and security, that's what
> people often want ... [helpful] words that allow
> them to deal with fuzzy ill-structured problems—in
> a procedural way. But we're into situations with
> the growth of technology and the rapidity of change
> where we don't have the ability to deal with these
> needs for clarity and security.

These remarks highlight a major dilemma. Organizations
desperately need people who are able to cope with change, even
if they don't quite enjoy it. Historically, the trend has been
toward creating a sense of stability and certainty. Many people
have come to see themselves as having a clear place in their organizations, whether in terms of their immediate job or career
path, and this has been encouraged by organizational and union
policies that stress the need for clearly defined responsibilities
and routes to seniority. Now, this trend needs to be reversed to
create a situation in which people recognize and accept change,
and rise to meet the challenges it brings. Debate on this issue
quickly focuses on the ability and motivation of people to cope
with new situations. In my research, some executives expressed
great optimism:

> You'd be surprised at the ingenuity of peo-
> ple in coping with new situations. [They] rise to
> the occasion. One of the problems is that for a long
> time [they] haven't had enough occasions to rise to.

> People, if they believe they are part of a
> change process, will be on their metal; they usually
> do their best.

mettle

Others were more cautious, emphasizing "the rigidities
arising from unionization" and the resistance from "bureaucratic
attitudes" and "fear of technology."

There is little that managers can do about resistance to change that has deep psychological roots, though there are major implications for our educational system. Nevertheless, an enormous amount can be done with respect to the management of change and its impact on current employee attitudes. Given the impact of new technologies, new forms of competition, and the periodic crises that seem to impact most organizations, it is imperative that corporations have a policy on their attitude toward change, on how it should be handled and on how it should influence the tenure of employees.

An organization's decision to "downsize" or restructure by terminating sections of its workforce can have a major impact on the loyalty of those who remain and on the corporate culture in general. It is difficult to relish change and retain a strong commitment to an organization if one's future employment is uncertain. In an era when even the most senior staff experience "the axe" and where multibillion-dollar companies terminate major portions of their workforce, who can feel secure?

This problem highlights a major dilemma for the organization that wants creative, committed employees while it remains flexible to meet new environmental challenges. For some organizations the solution lies in developing schemes that provide employment security, as opposed to job security: schemes that guarantee employees an income and a role in the organization, but not a specific role. In this way, security is defined in financial terms—rather than in terms of the right to discharge a particular set of duties or responsibilities—and the organization provides suitable retraining and development programs. This can do much to foster flexibility, but as a number of executives observed it requires that managers help employees to develop an evolving sense of their identity and potential role in the organization.

> To work off something as general as a sense of mission requires an openness on the part of the employees as to what their self images are. . . . We must have employees define themselves less [in

terms of] what their particular function is at a
given time, so they are not traumatized when we
want them to do another thing. And this goes for
the CEO right on down.

[Traditionally] people have had a concept
of their craft and a way of describing themselves.
. . . "This is what I do. I'm a such and such." [But]
now, we can't promise our staff, whether white- or
blue-collar, what they are going to do for twenty
years. We have to help them think differently about
their work life. Their work life involves being a
member of a team that produces a car, builds an
office, designs a system or whatever, where there is
no guaranty that they will do the same thing all the
time. [They] have to expect to . . . learn new skills
much more frequently.

One executive reported how his organization had struck
a particularly creative solution to the security-flexibility dilemma by treating all employees as full stakeholders in the organization and interpreting the problem of providing job security as
one of finding new business opportunities.

There's something negative about finding
ways of getting rid of people, rather than finding
ways of doing something new as a basis of growth.
We've made it a part of our mission to create employment—to find new business to support our
employees. And we ask them to be effective and
flexible in return. One of our specific strategies is
to try and empower individual staff to manage
their own skills and careers. We recognize that we
can't do this for them, and that it is *they* who can
make us a better organization. Under one scheme
we've set up a special project group comprising
twenty people. Anyone in the company can join
this group for six months and be exposed to many
aspects of the company. The only requirement is

that they can't return to their original job after the six months. The scheme promotes change and the philosophy that is necessary for the company to change. We've already changed 500 jobs over a two-year period.

For other organizations the solution to the security-flexibility problem is found in moving to a subcontracting arrangement where people work on specific but limited assignments for predefined rewards. The problems that arise in this instance lie in encouraging temporary employees to make contributions that have long-term significance and in building continuity.

Each of these approaches raises issues about the extent to which employees are to be viewed as stakeholders in the organization and how ownership issues and rewards are to be defined and resolved. Both approaches point to the importance of managerial skills that can help employees deal with ambiguity and change and trade unions in negotiating policies and principles that will help protect their members in a world where flexibility is at a premium.

Blending "Specialist" and "Generalist" Qualities

There has been long-standing debate about the merits of "generalists" and "specialists" and the profile of the ideal manager. The executives involved in my research heavily favored generalist abilities, but they tended to reject the either–or character of the generalist–specialist distinction. Instead, they felt that the modern executive needs *both* qualities. Complete specialism was seen as a problem in view of the diverse nature of the modern corporate environment. And generalism—"a good manager can manage anything"—was thought to ignore the fact that in today's environment there is absolutely no substitute for an intimate knowledge of the nature of one's business. One CEO expressed the situation in relation to his role:

You have to know your business in terms of *detailed* understanding. You have to have this. The generalist stuff is crap. Most executive skills may be generic, but to be effective you must know the details of the business with which you are dealing.

On balance, there was a feeling that specialist abilities are often overdeveloped and generalist abilities underdeveloped, and that to enrich the human resource base of our organizations, these abilities must be blended to achieve a broadening of skills and perspectives; a better appreciation of the relationship between the human and technical aspects of the manager's role; and a greater emphasis on the entrepreneurial and creative aspects of the management process.

Broadening Skills and Perspectives. Many employees enter organizations as specialists. But today's world often requires that they reach beyond their traditional skills and gain a wider appreciation of their role within their organization and of the organization's role in the outside world. Unfortunately, this development is often blocked. Some executives pointed to the technical myopia of many employees, including managers:

> I find that we have too many technicians, and not enough professionals. At some point you . . . require a person who has all the technical stuff. But the most crucial talent has to be a wider view of things and the ability to relay what he or she is doing to others.

The limited focus of employees who are "unable to grasp the whole," "to sort the wheat from the chaff," "to integrate present and future," and "to separate events from issues" was also seen as a problem. Considerable blame was placed on the way people are trained and educated and on the process of socialization and perception in the television age:

> Too many people are taught to be reductive rather than creative. Frequently they can write a 120-page paper on the perfect baked bean. Brilliant . . . but!!!

Most of the time you have someone who is extraordinarily capable of dealing with today's operations or someone who is very capable of dealing with the vision. But it's rare that you have both in one person.

You have to motivate as many people as possible in the organization to blend today and tomorrow in their approach to management. It's not just something that the CEO should do. It should [be done throughout] the organization.

In order to cope with change . . . especially in an international context, people have to know who they are. . . . There is nothing that leads to more insecurity than the absence of experience and a broadly based knowledge of the world. If you've had to move from a known environment to an unknown environment and have developed a capacity to cope with change, [there is much less] threat from the unknown.

Lasting issues are neglected in favor of the latest issues . . . and there is an orientation toward events as opposed to issues. I think it comes from the pressure of events [as the urgent squeezes out the important] . . . and from television. . . . If there is no event associated with [an issue], we don't have the modes of discourse to deal with it. Now, politics, for example, is a series of events, not a series of issues. . . . We are living in a world [dominated by events], where we constantly switch channels.

The executives who discussed these issues saw them as real problems having a major impact on organizations and requiring major initiatives—especially in the field of education—to put them right. But they also felt that one cannot wait for these initiatives to emerge. Each organization needs to encourage employees to examine how the blinders imposed by education, personal and social history, and technical training may block their overall ability and development and to remove them whenever possible.

Improving Relations Between the Human and Technical Aspects of the Manager's Role. The development of technical specialization has had a tendency to downgrade the importance of the human element in organizations. People are frequently appointed for their technical skills, with the *hope* that they also have good interpersonal skills. In the view of many executives involved in my research it is high time to redress the imbalance by making people critically aware of the importance of integrating the technical and human factors in management. The basic problems and some possible solutions were expressed in many ways:

> Motivating people—but we've got to find a better expression—has to be part of a manager's job description. Instead of saying this fellow is a good accountant, and to boot, he's good with people, we have to say there are two sides to this job—you have to be a class accountant or sales manager and a crack motivator. It will then emerge as a competency, not just as icing on the cake.

> I'm not suggesting that accountants are not important, that finance types are not important, or that computer specialists are not important. But, beyond that, to make the whole system work, you've got to have people who are people oriented, who are trying to understand humans, be they customers, workers, foreigners, the government, or whatever. Number crunching [is not enough]. It is the human side that [makes all the] differences these days.

> As more and more of the physical and technical aspects of a manager's role are routinized or removed through automation, the proportion of

time in which skills associated with the subjective
side of life are required increases. Dealing with people as people, getting the most out of them, and
helping them to do their jobs [becomes more and
more important]. Automation has made many jobs
less routine. Machines now have the routine jobs.
There is an enormous need for nurturing the management competencies that allow people to handle
the nonroutine. There is no manual for this, except
that of human relations. It's not just a question of
technical skills.

Such comments send a clear message about the importance of
the human side of a manager's job. The manager of the future
will be expected to stretch beyond the bounds of technical
competence and develop people skills as an essential ingredient
of the managerial role.

*Emphasizing the Entrepreneurial and Creative Aspects of
the Management Process.* Finally, it is necessary to achieve more
integration and balance between the operational and creative
sides of management. Increasingly, organizations need people
who can simultaneously operate within *and* think out of a mold:
production managers who combine their capacity for disciplined
work with a capacity to generate new ideas on the basis of this
experience; "creative idea types" who have the ability to make
their idea a reality through disciplined work; and so on. As one
executive put it, "the production manager whose head is in the
sand or the entrepreneurial person whose head is in the clouds
do little." What is needed is a blend of creativity and discipline,
of opportunity seeking and productive work. The ability to initiate and foster this synthesis is an important competency for
future management.

Managing in an Environment of Equals

The more organizations move toward the employment of
people valued for the knowledge and distinctive skills *they* bring
to the work situation, the more managers must move away from

directive styles of management. Relatively predictable situations, where the manager knows as much as the worker, can be supervised; however, this scenario is disappearing. Now, managers often find themselves in situations where their employees know more about the immediate job. In such situations, managers cannot function with any degree of competence unless they prove their worth as a *resource* to those they are "managing," whether as a "troubleshooter" with specialist knowledge or skills, a "sounding board," an idea generator, a coordinator, a team builder, a facilitator, or a motivator. This situation requires that we rethink the concept of manager. The disappearing middle levels of so many organizations bear testimony to this: under the impact of the new technology, team-based organizational designs, increased decentralization, and schemes for self-organization, management in the traditional sense is often no longer required.

Here is how some of the executives involved in my research described the skills and abilities required by the new style manager/orchestrator/facilitator. He or she must be able:

- "To help people on a day-to-day basis without supervising their work; [meaning] you have to have some method of being helpful at the generic level, without keeping track of the details"
- To act as "a resource person rather than a controller, cultivating relations so that staff will call you in when you are required"
- "To create and communicate a sense of vision and make decisions only when necessary, for example, as a troubleshooter, arbitrator, or hatchet man"
- To orchestrate, facilitate, and network—"to create conditions that allow things to happen, by finding opportunities, dislodging roadblocks, or acting on focal points that lead to desired action"
- To exercise "influencing skills" including those of conflict management and negotiation
- To engage in "team building" and develop other participative and collaborative skills

- "To work laterally and to launch and sustain joint ventures"
- "To deal with uncertainty and ambiguity at a fast speed"
- "To be sensitive to the soft as opposed to the hard, finite, technical sides of an issue"
- "To be intuitive and sensitive to nondeductive problem-solving methodologies"
- "To remain open and flexible, yet act decisively when required"
- "To motivate," "to inspire," "to turn people on," and "to avoid turning them off"
- "To make personal contact and empathize with employees so a bonding takes place"
- "To communicate key norms and values" and to nurture an appropriate sense of identity and corporate culture
- To lead *and* to participate: "to shape direction while remaining open to influence from others"

We find in this list, and in the discussion of remote management in Chapter Seven, a strong sense of the direction in which management may continue to move into the twenty-first century. Increasingly, organizations are dealing with new kinds of employees using new technologies and requiring new forms of management. Many of these required skills are more "female" than "male," perhaps signifying great opportunity for women in organizations. We have been through a phase of "macho management" in which a highly analytical, directive, "top-down" approach has dominated. Now we seem to be moving into a phase where more empathic, relationship-oriented approaches, based on cooperation rather than competition, are often more appropriate. Here, women often have the better record.

Education: A Continuous Process

Finally, we come to the issue of education. In an information society, knowledge is a key resource—some would say *the* key resource—and organizations must do everything they can to keep abreast of changing developments. Their effectiveness will be influenced by the quality of education in our society at large and by the initiatives they are able to develop on their own, such as in-house educational and training programs.

The various competencies identified in this book indicate some of the ways in which current management education programs can be refocused to concentrate on emerging requirements. The current changes in technologies, products, markets, and skills add to this agenda. Organizations of the future will need to develop greater skill in deciding where their money can be best spent, for the potential educational needs of employees are likely to outweigh the constraints of cost and time. In itself, this skill will be an important future competency for empowering and developing the human potential of an organization.

6

Promoting Creativity, Learning, and Innovation

Regardless of which industry you're in, and which market you are competing in . . . there are generic opportunities that have to be seized.

The situation regarding innovation varies from industry to industry. In some, discipline needs to be brought to creativity and change—to get the most out of it. In others that have been stable for years, the payoff is in being able to generate more lateral thinking.

These remarks capture how the need for innovation impacts different organizations. Without exaggeration, it is possible to say that *every* organization should be concerned with its capacity to innovate; however, the requirements for innovation vary from one organization to another. For some, innovation may be comfortably confined to doing more effectively what one is already doing. For others it may well dominate the spirit of an enterprise influencing every aspect of organizational functioning. In either case, it is important to pay attention to the managerial competencies that can help to generate innovation and channel it effectively. In this chapter, we discuss these competencies in terms of the following themes: developing an appropriate corporate culture; encouraging people to learn and be creative; and striking a balance between chaos and control.

Developing an Appropriate Corporate Culture

In the management of innovation, it is very important to create a climate, or corporate culture, in which value is placed on the ability to learn, to change, and generally to develop and promote new ideas. This may state the obvious, but the reality is that in many organizations, important ingredients of corporate practice encourage the reverse. Organizational structures and pyramidal lines of command often send subtle and not so subtle cues that people should maintain the status quo. Corporate politics may stifle new lines of development. Reward systems may encourage people not to make mistakes. And so on.

Organizations that have a good track record in innovation treat the matter very seriously and make the process central to corporate life. As reflected by one chief executive from a highly innovative company:

> Innovation is a big word for us. It's in the mission statement, and is a key driving force. One of the things that is just gut wrenching . . . is the idea of any competitor ever doing anything ahead of us with innovation. If you list the last twenty innovations in our industry, nineteen are ours. Three years ago we ran out of frontiers and, all of a sudden, the business became temporarily fixed. Depression took over.

Innovation is the lifeblood of this organization and runs in the veins of key employees. The organization selects people who want to be part of an innovative enterprise, and encourages the kind of self-questioning and development that keep innovation alive and well. In other organizations, innovation takes more of a background role—it takes place in the R&D department, but nowhere else—and has limited impact on corporate affairs because the rest of the employees are not primed to relish the excitement and problems of potential change. The following remarks, offered by senior executives whose organizations are struggling to become more flexible and innovative, speak to aspects of this problem:

> The culture of my organization tends to block innovation because the dominant values are those of control.

> One of the real problems [in my organization] is to find ways of creating a cultural transition from a situation dominated by senior executives who have grown up with the business in a different context into the present era where we face vastly different problems. We now have more competition than ever . . . and are going through a quantum change. One of our problems is to change our traditions and ways of operating . . . so that we can engage in the new battles.

> Organizations change over time, and you often end up with people who are stewards instead of builders. How do you change that [attitude] so they are not stewards?

The challenge of creating a corporate culture that is responsive to the need for innovation is a key management task. The methods for generating the sense of "adventure" and ability to step into the unknown, or motivating employees to take a more proactive attitude toward challenges and problems, will vary with the organization. There is no exact recipe; however, the executives involved in my research did feel that there are some ingredients that are useful in many situations.

Cultivating a Winning Attitude

> I have always been a competitor . . . and I like to be part of a winning team . . . . So I say for [my company], "I want to win." You have to get a consensus around winning and improving. I think that any organization that thinks it has all the right things in the right place at the right time is already on the decline, because an organization is dynamic, and competition is dynamic. Of course, you don't win at all costs. I want [my team] to play

with a certain decorum, a certain style, a certain poise. I want to be proud of them. I want them to share a vision by which they can win. And this is very important. I want them to win, but not at all costs.

Buying into Change

All you have to do is buy into change and be productive . . . into greater innovation in every workstation in the corporation. That is all you have to buy into. You don't have to understand what the future is going to hold in terms of specific requirements . . . [that can be] figured out as a supplementary exercise.

Creating a Sense of Optimism

You must create a sense of optimism and the feeling that people *can* influence things.

One of the basic premises must be that you can influence the future. You can motivate it. You can get where you want to go.

You must create a culture that believes in itself.

Adding Value

The approach in our organization is to pack our products with as much value to the customer as possible. We recognize that in searching for ways to add value we can create a competitive edge . . . it helps make us unique.

Encouraging Self-Questioning

In my organization we legitimize self-questioning [and constructive debate]. We have discussions focusing on our worst fears, our highest hopes, our strengths, and our weaknesses. As you go through this process you make an assessment of reality. And you build from there. That helps legitimize the philosophy of "let's get it on the table": How do the customers see us? What do our members think of us? What is the feedback? If you get all that stuff on the table, it legitimizes a process that can become constructive, because, at the bottom of it all is: "Okay, what are we going to do about this, this, this, and this? And where do we want to be three years from now?"

Creating a corporate culture that resonates with the demands facing an organization is what counts! In the words of one CEO:

Nirvana occurs when you can match your shadow, not what other people think . . . when you are nicely in sync with your own strengths.

Management of innovation must build around this idea, fostering the corporate ethos that enhances required strengths and energizes people to pursue desirable futures.

Encouraging Learning and Creativity

A vibrant corporate culture creates an effective context for innovation; however, much more can be done to foster learning and creativity on a continuous basis.

Brainstorming and Creative Thinking

A number of executives described their success with brainstorming sessions and how this technique provides "a simple and powerful tool" for opening up the creative process, even if it is used only on the occasional executive retreat or special meeting. One of them described his views in the following terms:

What we need to do in our organizations is
to generate and raise brainstorming to a more important activity. You need to get people in a room
and say "We will suspend critical judgment. You
are not responsible for any foolish comments you
make. For a couple of days, let's just let it hang
out!" This process needs to be made a part of
everybody's job, [generating] a basket of ideas out
of which the visionary can say: "Oh, yes, this is
something that sounds [promising]."

When this kind of session becomes part of business operations, an organization can gather considerable momentum. But
in unfavorable circumstances it can run into difficulty because
people may feel uncomfortable in breaking their usual mode
of behavior. As one executive reported:

I have tried to run sessions like that with
operations managers, and it's an impossible task.
First, they focus on exactly what they have always
done, unless you do ten [sessions] in a row. Then,
the tenth one [often] starts to be productive. [But]
it is so discouraging for the first nine. You don't
get anywhere. But the fact that it's not working
shows that you may be on the right track. Because
the more resistance you get, the more likely it is
that this is what you need to be doing.

Other executives mentioned the importance of trying to
generate "lateral thinking" to find new angles on old problems
and to open new lines of development. Much benefit was seen in
processes that attempt to connect different organizational domains, for example, by using technologies for one product to
create initiatives in relation to others. One chief executive described how his organization created success

by allowing a "new boy" to walk into the business
and to see it with new eyes, gathering and synthe-

sizing options, linking new ideas and technologies, and pulling it all together so that it worked.

Other executives emphasized the importance of encouraging people to focus on ideas rather than data:

> [In my strategic planning] I want a very open process. So I say to each division, "Let's be frank about it. I want as few numbers as possible, as much writing as possible. I want concepts, alternatives, and directions."

> We need to give people special assignments, both in our educational system and in our organizations, where they are not permitted to bring [in any data], to focus on pure "think pieces." They should be given the exercise of thinking.

Another chief executive described how he had attempted to sharpen creativity and critical thinking by encouraging employees to generate an idea, explain the concept to someone else to test its robustness and then to find someone who is willing to sponsor the idea as a policy option. This practice builds informally on processes that have been highly institutionalized in companies where idea generators are linked with "sponsors" or "product champions" and where formal review mechanisms exist to evaluate and allocate funds to promising projects.

In many organizations the pressures are such that the requirements of the now take precedence over those of the future. Short-term orientations dominate as top executives are "driven by quarterly reports" or the regular cycle of board meetings; little time is left to work on the future or to develop in-depth ideas about the present. These functions often are delegated to specialist or middle-level executives who are often subject to the same time pressures and short-term orientations. The result is no time for true creativity and exploration.

The ability to *make* time for these processes is very much connected with the corporate culture. If pressure and value are placed on "producing today" and "rewarding for today," the future is shortchanged. Of significance here is the faith placed in the continuing commitment of employees. As one executive observed, at the heart of the matter, many corporations feel deep down that there is no real long-term payoff in allowing unstructured time, or that to do so may leave a manager open to charges of being too loose, of not being on top of the job:

> The problem is that if people are taking time off, and something goes wrong, they will be seen as "goofing off." But there is another explanation as well. I think that companies don't believe that their employees are committed to their organizations, and that's why they don't want to give them time to do things that are not productive in a concrete way. The way you get ahead [nowadays] is by going from one organization to another, and cutting a better deal. That makes senior management unhappy about being loose with people's time, because they don't believe that they are going to put that time to work for the organization over a long career. I am not just talking about senior people not allowing their juniors to do this. I am talking about senior people not allowing themselves to do it.

The allocation of time for creative work, the ability to ensure that this time results in the generation of ideas and opportunities that resonate with the challenges facing an organization, and the ability to keep key people are competencies critical to the management of innovation. Often, people have the capacity to think critically and productively, but they must be encouraged and supported in this endeavor.

Embracing Variety

For an organization to generate *appropriate* innovation it is vital to build around the principle of incorporating sufficient variety into its idea generation and decision-making processes. There is a well known law in cybernetics—the law of requisite variety—which states that for any system to adapt to its external environment, its internal controls must incorporate the variety found in that environment. If one reduces the variety inside, the system is unable to cope with the variety outside. The point seems an obvious one but in fact many organizations try to function by doing the reverse. For example, in establishing planning teams or project groups, organizations often filter diversity by removing potentially disruptive elements: selecting people who think alike, proceeding quickly in the absence of awkward members, and so on. The process results in quick plans and actions, but these soon meet resistance in the face of reality. Creativity thrives on the tension created by diversity, and it is essential that steps be taken to ensure that organizations build enough tension and variety into processes where innovation is required.

Many successful firms have learned the value of this principle through simple practices. For example, many firms find that it is often much more effective to establish customer "focus groups" to discuss strengths and weaknesses of services or products than to rely on abstract surveys or research. It is often much more effective to negotiate with external protagonists and "work around the negatives" *before* a decision is made, rather than fight the opposition afterward and thereby incur expensive delays. It is often much more effective to begin a decision-making process by casting a broad net, involving unusual people, exploring unusual ideas, and being open to the influence of variety, rather than forcing a narrow point of view or pet approach that "must be made to succeed at all costs." The principles seem obvious, but the tendency to find the quickest and easiest solutions often dominates practice, eliminating key issues and tensions that could enrich the decision process and the effectiveness of the resulting actions.

To embrace variety managers need special skills in negotiation, consensus building, and conflict management, and a philosophy that encourages people to deal with issues rather than bury them. Many of these qualities also need to be built into the corporate culture.

Shock and Surprise

A variation on the variety theme: shock and surprise can do much to foster required innovation. Sometimes, shock can be so large and traumatic that it paralyzes; however, if the means can be found to mobilize an organization's response to the unexpected, the consequences can be beneficial.

Alternatives to Hierarchy

Hierarchy stifles debate. There is an organizational pattern that supports challenging people, helps with innovation, helps with creativity. It is anything but the pyramid, or any kind of hierarchical structure.

There is something about large organizations that breeds conservatism and the avoidance of risk. Big business stifles initiative, since the tendency toward rationalization leads managers to want to see the total package before decisions are made. Smaller organizations have an advantage here, since there is much more room for incremental approaches.

There is an opportunity within our grasp at the moment, because of technology, to break up some of our big bureaucratic organizations. When you get big organizations, it is difficult to break the rules. But if you get down to smaller units, you can afford more flexibility in a structure that encourages more entrepreneurship.

Flatten the organization, and get self-organization to occur, where managers facilitate, allowing the specific steps to come from the employees most directly involved.

Many large innovative companies have little skunk works, or little task forces and groups. I think that innovation is much easier to come by in a small group than in a massive organization. So, if we are in big companies, how do we set up the organization in such a way that you give freedom to small groups of people to develop and be innovative? I think that is crucial.

I am leaning toward saying that the answer [to creating flexibility] is to fragment your organization enormously so that the operative units can, in fact, work in a very short time frame. We have to look at how that can happen. Is there some way to run [a large company] with very, very small units that can behave that way, and still maintain the fiduciary control that the senior staff is obligated to maintain? And then you may not have to worry so much about the long run, because as the world changes, some of these units will react, and some will survive, and some will find themselves anachronistic, and [the organization] will act as a bunch of small companies.

I know an organization that operates that way. As soon as something becomes too big it is spun off, but there is an umbilical cord that keeps it in some way connected.

If you confuse healthy growth with size, you've got a real problem.

The quotations send strong messages. In a nutshell:

- Create flatter organizations
- Generate flexibility and freedom
- Develop structures that promote entrepreneurship and risk taking
- Build around small groups
- Decentralize and give autonomy to the employees most directly involved

- Find ways of controlling from a distance
- Grow large while retaining the advantages of being small

These ideas can help to shape the design of innovative organizations. And developments in information technology and the principles of self-organization and remote management are helping to make them a reality. Large bureaucratic organizations have a hard time innovating and are being replaced by more fluid organic forms that build on the intelligence and skills of their people. The tasks of creating such organizations and managing in a more open context are among the most important competencies required in the years ahead. They are examined later in this chapter and in Chapter Seven.

Improving Lateral Interactions

One of the most important ingredients for successful operation in flat organizations is the ability to create effective lateral interaction. The success of team-based approaches to organization is well known, and the multidisciplinary project team has established itself as a basic building block in any organization concerned with innovation and the solution of complex problems.

However, to create effective teamwork, particularly of a multidisciplinary kind, certain requirements must be met. First, and foremost, the people involved must be able to talk and work with each other. This may be stating the obvious, but in many organizations functional divisions and technical demarcations often block successful interaction. To overcome this, departmental and other artificial barriers must be dissolved, and more attention must be given to the effective use of meetings and electronic forms of coordination. The executives involved in my research were able to offer success stories in the use of electronic mail, but many believed that considerable attention still needs to be devoted to the development of competencies such as how to conduct meetings and basic communications skills. While electronics can facilitate information exchange, personal interaction through videoconferencing or conventional meetings is as important as ever in "managerial cheerleading," in coalition building, in adding an extra dimension to raw information, and in "getting people on the same wavelength." A number of executives from organizations at which team-based action is a way of life suggested some important means of helping to make meetings more effective:

> A part of the problem is that more and more people think that they have an interest in a certain subject, and if anyone is going to talk about it they've got to be there. As more and more people do that, you get bigger and bigger meetings, and the bigger they get, the less effective they get, because they're less focused—because each participant has a particular viewpoint to get across. [But] a sense of common purpose will mitigate people's fear about not participating in meetings where they have a stake in what is going on. Trust [is important]. The smaller the unit, the more prepared you are not to be there, oddly enough, because the more you feel that no one is going to take advantage of you. But when the faceless mask of "corporate planning" is going to deal with your side of the company, boy, you've got your spies working on it, and boy, you'd better be there.

> The traditional response to a communications problem—when things go haywire—is to send more memos and hold more meetings. But [the better response] is to ask whether people can see where the whole is going . . . and if there is a basis for trust to grow. That is the only way communications will really improve.

Technology can help in the exchange of information. But the norms, values, and expectations that shape a corporate culture influence what information is exchanged and how it is used. If we understand this, we have the means to improve communications within an organization, by improving the *context* in which they occur.

However good the communications, however dedicated the employees, however cohesive the organization appears, conflicts are inevitable. This is especially true of innovative organizations. Innovation is spurred by enthusiasm and strong opinion, and opinions often diverge. The skills of conflict management are thus crucial in ensuring that such conflict is constructive rather than destructive and that operations are kept moving. Conflict does not have to be overt. Often it lies beneath the surface, stifling projects to a slow death. It is thus important that managers read and handle the hidden tensions, as well as the more obvious conflicts arising from excess enthusiasm, dogmatic opinion, careerism, or outright competition.

An Experimental Bias

Innovation demands risk taking and a proactive "let's see if it works" attitude. There must be a supportive corporate culture that encourages staff to experiment. This demands a tolerance for errors that arise when dealing with new situations (as opposed to mistakes that should have been avoided) and a view of accountability that supports this. In many organizations, error is punished in ways that lead employees to avoid putting themselves at risk, squashing all entrepreneurial initiative. Managers must always be aware of this possibility and work hard to promote the proactive, risk-taking ethos so important for innovation.

Time Out

Innovation requires time out: an opportunity to break the routine, distance oneself, and work on something completely different. Insights often come from "out of the blue" when you least expect them and can be invoked by chance connections of many kinds. Yet this flexible use of time runs against commonly held work norms. While groups may be given time for structured or unstructured creative thinking—as in quality circles or brainstorming sessions—it is far less common to extend this opportunity to individuals.

Creating the Right Rewards

As part of this support, it is vitally important that an appropriate reward system be established. The organization that rewards mediocrity cultivates the mediocre and forces its best talent to go elsewhere. There is something dynamic and immediate about innovation, and effective systems of reward must also have this character. Many successful innovative firms recognize special contributions symbolically, as well as materially, so that all employees are aware of the kind of performance that is valued and appreciated.

Special attention must also be given to the problem of motivating long-term as well as short-term thinking in employees, an issue expressed by one CEO in the following terms:

> To get entrepreneurs into our structures we have to find ways of encouraging entrepreneurship and rewarding people for [having] tomorrow's attitudes. [By] rewarding people for just fitting in— for reading the rules of today's game and "going through the hoops" in a ritualistic way—we stifle the potential for development.

Attention must also be paid to the problem of developing reward systems that recognize superior individual or group contributions, while avoiding a divisive impact on the rest of the organization. Sometimes innovation rests on individual efforts, which call for individual rewards. More often, however, it is a group effort, a web of crucial but low-profile contributions. If reward systems rupture this web, future performance may be harmed.

Striking a Balance Between Chaos and Control

> There is a fine line between tough controls and chaos. You have to encourage creativity, so that

people can contribute to their job. But there have
to be some controls. How do you give people freedom, yet have some control? How can you give a
manager thousands of miles away the freedom to
run an organization, yet have the proper controls
that will give you the early warning systems if
there are any problems? Striking that balance is a
critical task of management.

As this CEO suggests, a key dilemma in the management
of innovation is the need to strike a balance between the openness that encourages creativity and the rigor of control. Employees must be given sufficient freedom, but their activities
must resonate with the needs of the organization.

The executives involved in my research project were at
one in emphasizing that one has to find alternatives to the traditional methods of control, such as hierarchy, rules, and narrow job descriptions. In particular, they stressed the need to set
guidelines and parameters rather than allocate specific duties
and manage through the creation of shared values rather than
through close control. For example:

I find that a job description is anti-innova-
tion. If you let the person make the job, instead of
the job define the person, I think you get better results. I am convinced of that. But there is a very
fine balance between this and chaos.

If you train people to live a life that is gov-
erned by rules, eventually you are going to train
them out of their ability to do anything else. You
squeeze initiative out.

There has to be enough structure, enough focusing, enough support to let [one's staff] develop
and flourish. And then the trick is to keep match-
ing mandates with the competencies and experience of the persons [involved]. When you try and

fit everybody into one mold—here is a job description for all accountants regardless of experience—
you get mismatches. If you have very confident
people, you need energetic, developing, professional leadership. You don't want a lot of rules and
regulations to get in the way.

Whether you are running a bureaucratic organization or one that runs on values or folklore,
there has to be accountability. In my organization
there is great emphasis on what is valued. There is
a whole culture around *what* is wanted and *how*
things should be done.

There is great pressure in many organizations to create
accountability by developing systems of rules. As one executive
put it, it can be very embarrassing if one cannot point to a clear,
orderly system when asked how something is done. But this
pressure must be resisted if innovation is to be sustained. One
needs to understand general principles. One needs some system
of accountability. Nevertheless, it is much better to fulfill these
requirements by creating systems of values through which employees can share and understand the mission and general parameters that guide action. The ability to find ways of creating this
form of control is an important managerial competency.

7

Developing Skills
in Remote Management

〰〰〰 We are moving into an age where the skills of "remote management" are going to be in great demand. The impact of electronic technology, the desire to reduce overheads, and the need to increase flexibility of operations are promoting decentralization. Large centralized hierarchies are giving way to flatter networks in smaller enterprises. In the process, many middle management positions are being eliminated and those that remain are being changed to fill new roles.

As I noted in Chapter Five, the modern manager frequently works in an environment of equals and interacts with networks of self-organizing groups rather than being in charge of a chain of command. This kind of manager—like the senior executives running "middleless organizations," needs to find ways of managing through a form of remote control—designing the parameters of the system, sensing when help is needed, and initiating appropriate support. In this chapter I explore this challenge by focusing on different aspects of the trend toward decentralization and sketching some of the new managerial styles and philosophies that are emerging.

Helicopter Management

Some organizations are disbanding large cadres of centralized staff and distributing functions that were once the preserve of headquarters among the operating units. This process creates decentralized organizations comprising loose networks of semiautonomous enterprises held together with minimal direct control. These units are given parameters within which they operate and are monitored on the basis of results. Planning can proceed from the bottom up; headquarters ensures that the plans agree with the organization's overarching vision and exercises ultimate financial control. Entrepreneurship is thus built into the operating units, which retain the autonomy necessary to operate speedily and flexibly and remain open to the changing requirements of the market.

Such an approach demands a specific set of skills at the very top of the organization, and at the divisional levels. At the top, the strategic leadership and positioning competencies discussed earlier need to be combined with early warning systems that indicate when attention is required without eroding the autonomy of unit managers. Imagine the chief executive and central staff operating as helicopter pilots:

> You must have a remote type of management facility—the Europeans call it the helicopter principle—where you hover like a helicopter over the scene. If something goes wrong, you can come down and resolve it, but essentially you operate at a distance, and let the operation go. This competence of remote management is very different from that of on-site management.

At divisional levels, executives must combine entrepreneurial skills with the ability to work under this helicopter control, recognizing and adhering to the wider corporate identity when necessary. As one of the main purposes in moving toward a decentralized system is distribution of autonomy to the separate units, the entrepreneurial aspects are critical. In many cases, the units operate as separate businesses, giving entrepreneurial initiative full rein. In other cases, especially where business units are closely linked in name and product with the central organization, entrepreneurship must be tempered by the need to sustain and enhance the overall corporate identity. Here, blending with the central organization is paramount.

Managing Through an Umbilical Cord

Another related approach to decentralization often cited by the executives involved in my research is found in those organizations where the philosophy of "growing large while remaining small" is achieved through creation of identical units more or less held together by a clearly articulated corporate philosophy or "blueprinting system." Under this system, when a business unit or factory grows to a certain size, further growth can be achieved only by establishment of a new satellite unit or factory. Each group of units or factories is permitted to grow to a specific size; thereafter, growth occurs through establishment of a new group. The process corresponds to organic growth: once a cell reaches maturity it has to split. The total organization grows by creating a constellation of similar organizations and suborganizations, each operating autonomously within the context of a central corporate philosophy. Each group of organizations within the system may be a self-sufficient "corporation within a corporation" in that it has its own finance, marketing, research, and industrial relations, and the capacity to spawn yet another corporation.

This system builds on a form of remote management exercised through a strongly developed corporate philosophy and sense of corporate culture. This linking of values and beliefs, along with the flow of services each group provides its constituent units, serves as an umbilical cord, creating a high degree of unity in the context of a highly decentralized style of management. The principle has great merit and potential in creating networks of small-scale organizations that allow for a variety of contributions and managerial abilities. In such a system there is room both for skilled entrepreneurs who aspire to build their own group of organizations *and* for managers with more limited aspirations and abilities. This is important, as there is real danger in building an organization around superstars. As one executive cautioned:

> Building a model [for one's organization]
> that requires a lot of entrepreneurship is, I think,

looking for grief. What you should be looking for are the competencies necessary for average managers to run tiny units that are hanging off the side [of the larger organization]. Not [everyone] is a gifted entrepreneur. There are going to be a lot of average people, and we have to have places for them to manage. If we want the small unit model to survive, we had better structure it so there's adequate supervision. The whole idea that entrepreneurship is going to be able to save North American industry is great, but there aren't that many entrepreneurs around.

The "growing large while remaining small" approach has room for the superstars, but it is also realistic in that it builds on the creativity and hard work of other managers who wish to find a niche at an intermediate level, perhaps as the manager of a single factory or business unit.

Promoting Self-Organization

Another way of decentralizing and promoting remote management is found in the trend toward self-organization. In the past, management has been conceived primarily as a process of external control. The manager has been "in charge." Now, the trend is toward self-organization or self-management, replacing the large numbers of middle managers with smaller numbers of orchestrator/facilitator/managers. This trend is manifested in the increasing use of quality circles, autonomous work groups, and project-driven organizations designed to build requisite skills into work units so that these units function with minimal external intervention. The role of the independent manager in such situations becomes that of a general resource, a troubleshooter in exceptional circumstances, and a "boundary spanner" or networker linking the group in question to the wider organization.

This organizational design represents a decisive break with past management principles. The traditional bureaucratic

approach developed through the fragmentation of work processes; different functions were allocated to different people.
With the new approach, integration is the rule. People are given
multifunctional roles, thus creating the flexibility that allows
self-organization to occur.

This approach helps to make the most of an organization's human resources by encouraging employees to use their
intelligence and abilities to full effect. The bureaucratic approach has often stultified human achievement by assuming
that employees are less able and resourceful than they actually
are and causing employees to operate at the lower levels expected of them. This issue attracted the attention of a number
of executives involved in my research project. They argued that
organizations tend to attract the kind of employee they deserve
and approaches to management that allow for growth and development will generally produce growth and development. The
problem facing many traditional organizations was summarized
by an executive discussing the banking system:

> Why do [many] banks manage to employ
> rigid local bank managers who follow a manual in
> how they treat the customer and in what loan ap-
> plications they accept? Is it because they couldn't
> get 2500 real bankers into the branches [and thus
> resorted to the rulebook], or is it that they didn't
> . . . give them a chance to become real bankers and
> made them all clerks?

By fostering self-organization and styles of remote management, organizations can help to overcome these problems
and do much to develop their capacities for innovation and
change.

Managing Ambiguity

Management of self-organizing units in a hands-off style
demands special qualities. Many managers are very action oriented in a hands-on way and find it very frustrating to hold

back and pass initiative and control to others. Yet this restraint is required if decentralized modes of organization are to operate effectively. The hands-on approach to management is often linked with a demand for clarity. The hands-off or remote approach demands an ability to deal with ambiguity. Future managers will need to develop their skills and tolerance levels in dealing with loosely structured situations. They will need to "read" how situations are developing and when intervention is necessary. And they will need to intervene in ways that empower rather than weaken the people and units being managed.

To acquire such skills, managers must be aware of the importance of feedback systems that keep one informed without creating direct operational control. It is necessary to detect those warning signs that indicate help may be needed, either to overcome inaction or to manage undesirable trends. In complex situations the threat of paralysis is always present. Situations can change so quickly or unexpectedly and place people in situations in which they are unsure of what action to take. The remote manager must look for this paralysis and find ways to overcome it. Buck passing, scapegoating, and overdelegation are warning signs:

> You have to watch for signs that suggest one's staff are engaging in too much delegation—either laterally or downward. Many people may hide behind the ideas that they are "developing their younger staff" or "have insufficient time to do a particular project," when the truth is that they really don't quite know what to do. Rather than deal with the problems and ambiguity they face they pass them to someone else. The ability to overcome this kind of paralysis is a real competency.

The remote manager must also become skilled in shaping or redirecting the energies of staff through the management of values, rather than through direct control. He or she must be able to tolerate the ambiguity of influencing situations symbolically in a "second-hand" manner, by shaping the context within which the desired results can occur. This may be as simple as affirmation and communication of a set of values that guide action and within which units have the freedom to operate.

Empowering staff to be competent—motivating *them* to mobilize their own abilities to deal with difficult situations—is another problem. Future managers will have to become as skilled in the art of empowerment as traditional managers are skilled in exercising direction and control.

Finally, there are the problems encountered in transforming one's own values, watching for potential regressions, and ensuring that top managers are able to live with the remote management style. These problems cannot be overemphasized, because direct control is often more attractive and more comfortable than the ambiguity of remote management, especially under pressure. Many of the potential difficulties and dilemmas are highlighted in the following remarks:

> Many organizations have tended to be successful because of very tight centralized control. They have tended to stick to their knitting for generations and have been very successful. Now, the modern demand to become more market driven requires that they be fragmented and cut into smaller units. But the whole paternalistic attitude of senior management has got to change in order for this new structure to work. Many organizations have no mechanism to allow the transition to occur in an orderly way, and desperately need an intervention that will help them to manage this.

> The people at the top often can't let go because their concept of being organized is linked to controlling and monitoring constituent units. It's very threatening to let the units go where they will. But there are means of holding these units together in a nonstructural way. One can use mission, values, and beliefs to create unity and coherence in a way that will allow constituent units to find their own place within the whole.

There is also a fear that the people at the bottom will not be driven to the same excellence in decision making as those at the top.

These problems add to the tension and ambiguity of the remote manager's role and are challenges that must be confronted.

Making Specialist Staff Client Oriented

Another aspect of the move toward flatter decentralized organizations is found in how specialist support services—such as strategic planning, MIS, and human resource management—have become more responsive to the needs of line managers. In the past, there has been a tendency for these services to become highly departmentalized, with professional and departmental goals and priorities often becoming ends in themselves. As a result, they have failed to serve the needs of their clients.

The specialist often sees things in terms of programs of work for his or her department, rather than in terms of line effectiveness. We need to find ways of making specialists more client oriented.

Professional specialists often want ideal solutions or systems designs, and can often see a five-year solution. But the pace of change will not allow this kind of time. Line departments usually want actions and solutions now, even if they're not ideal. A much more ad hoc approach is necessary than the specialists are prepared to provide.

One of the key problems in my organization rests in integrating systems of support into line management. For example, MIS has developed "the 10th floor" as a separate function with a strong culture.

Many executives spoke strongly about the need to overcome these problems and reported on a number of initiatives that can help to make these services much more flexible and client oriented. For example, one CEO of an international corporation described how he had made strategic planning a bottom-up line function, thus using the knowledge of the people most closely involved with products and customers. As a result of this decentralization, the corporate headquarters could be reduced to a very small staff. Another executive offered the following thoughts:

> I may be overstating it but we should get rid of the strategic planners and say to operating executives "There are two aspects to your job—today and tomorrow!" Planners should become process people and catalysts rather than people who produce plans. We should make people better planners. Today and tomorrow are much closer than we usually think. Responding to the longer term in product strategy, market strategy, or whatever is usually rooted in a better understanding of your customer or your market. There is no discontinuity between today and tomorrow.

Yet another executive reported how his company made the MIS function more client oriented by mandating the MIS department to become a quasi-independent business with the goal of generating at least 75% of its projects from outside the parent organization within a five-year period. The parent was no longer obliged to use the MIS branch, forcing MIS to compete and in the process become much more client centered.

> There is a totally different mindset and motivation between the MIS person inside a company and the MIS consultant outside. The latter is user driven. He sees the utility to the user as paramount and recognizes that if satisfaction is not provided he won't be paid and won't get any more jobs. He is thus often forced to make judgments and trade-offs that the inside person is not prepared to make.

The internal MIS person is usually more of a purist. He doesn't want to screw up and has a "no rush, no error" mentality [which in the present degree of flux is impractical]. Under the new system, MIS realizes that it has to meet our needs on a system, because otherwise we will go outside.

The aim in all these initiatives is to create a much more flexible and needs-oriented use of specialist resources and to dissolve the professional dominance that often arises as staff departments become entrenched in favorite approaches and mindsets. In the process, these initiatives also increase the demand for remote management skills. Line managers need these skills in order to orchestrate, facilitate, and coordinate the activities of their professional staffs. And the managers of professional services must develop these skills in order to face the challenge of linking, motivating, and developing staff who are widely dispersed and working in situations in which reporting relations and the usual departmental lines of authority have been radically altered or dissolved. Organizations that wish to be flexible and innovative will become more and more dependent on the art and craft of remote management.

8

Harnessing the Creative Power of Information Technologies

I heard someone tell a story about the high-tech industry a while ago, and it went something like this: "It's as if the computer industry is in a large airplane traveling 600 mph at 35,000 feet. Everyone else is on the ground, and being left behind at a rapid rate. The computer people in the plane are separated from the intense cold outside by thick plastic windows; they're remote from the everyday problems on the ground. They're just selling their stuff and letting the customers get on with it."

This comment from a CEO grasps an important aspect of current developments. Technological progress is occurring at a fantastic rate. The computer buffs are able to keep up, but those on the implementation side are left standing still by the incredible pace of change. The consequences of the new technology are unfolding in complex and unexpected ways, and influencing virtually every aspect of organization. It is as if we are riding a roller coaster:

We have the problem of getting on board *and* staying on board. The pace of change is such that no sooner than one is on top of a situation, the technology changes, and one has to think about starting over again.

There can be little doubt that information technology is among the most important forces reshaping the modern organization. As illustrated in Figure 5, the consequences of the technology—in the form of microcomputers, robotics, and other electronic communications—are transforming the way work is performed and, eventually, will demand that we rethink basic principles of organization and management. In this chapter, I discuss the numerous ways in which the new technology will reshape managerial competencies, focusing on creative use of the technology, problems of planning, information management, and software.

Creative Use of Information Technology

The new technology can allow us to do old things better, but it can also allow us to do new things in new ways. One of the major challenges facing managers now and in the future is to use the technology to develop new products and services; new network concepts of organization; new modes of work design; new styles of decision making; flexible, smaller-scale operations; a new literacy; and new attitudes toward change.

New Products and Services

Microprocessing and other information technologies have already exerted a major impact on the design of products and services. Three aspects are particularly important.

First is the trend toward "smart products." In this age of the microchip, products are being given brains. Photocopiers, typewriters, telephone systems, watches, electronic calculators, automobiles, and other goods have built-in computers that provide them with new capacities. Product concepts and design can thus evolve extremely rapidly.

Second is the trend toward multipurpose products. At one time products were manufactured with a single function in mind. Now, they are designed to serve many purposes. Thus, telephones are conferencing systems, modems for data transmission, and decision-making systems that can reroute calls. Televisions are newspapers, sources of entertainment, display terminals,

Figure 5. The Transformative Impact of Information Technology.

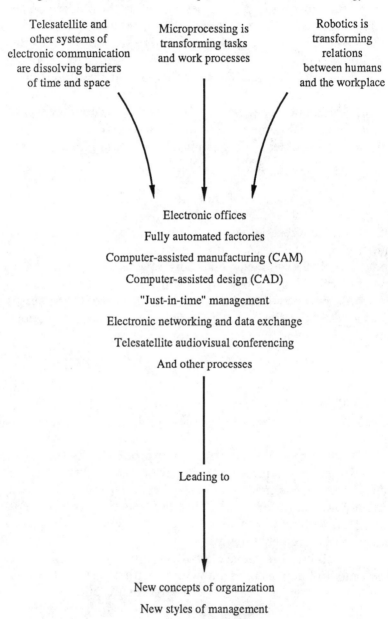

Telesatellite and other systems of electronic communication are dissolving barriers of time and space

Microprocessing is transforming tasks and work processes

Robotics is transforming relations between humans and the workplace

Electronic offices

Fully automated factories

Computer-assisted manufacturing (CAM)

Computer-assisted design (CAD)

"Just-in-time" management

Electronic networking and data exchange

Telesatellite audiovisual conferencing

And other processes

Leading to

New concepts of organization

New styles of management

New managerial competencies

and video-stereo systems. Banks, insurance companies, trust companies, real estate firms, and other institutions are being transformed into "one-stop financial centers." And so on.

A third trend is the emergence of "peripherally driven systems." Increasingly, air-conditioning and heating in large offices, television viewing, expenditure approvals on credit cards, airline reservations, and other transactions and services are "user driven" from remote locations. Such systems were once controlled from a central point; now, they are controlled from many points, and develop in many directions simultaneously.

These and related developments have important implications for future managerial competencies. First, it is clear that no organization can take the nature of its products and services for granted. It is thus necessary to develop capacities for rethinking the nature of one's industry and understanding how the capacities generated by new technology can be linked to user requirements, so that products and services develop holistically to serve *systems* of consumer needs, rather than single functions.

Second, the new technology is dramatically influencing product life cycles, which in many industries and services are becoming shorter and shorter. This has implications for product design and poses a strategic choice as to whether products should be designed for a short life or in ways that allow for evolution in the consumer's hands. With respect to the latter, it may be possible to design products that evolve through replacement of old components with more advanced components or of one programmed electronic chip with another.

The reduction in product life cycles also has many organizational implications. For example, how can organizations develop the competencies necessary to move rapidly from R&D into effective production and marketing and to generate an adequate return on capital within a very short payback period? As payback periods in some industries are as short as six months, and certainly no longer than eighteen months to three years, it is often difficult to make the right judgments on product development, especially because this phase can last from two to six years. The problems are great:

We've been faced with the problem of having products where the product doctrine was virtually obsolete before it hit the market, and that was a culmination of six or seven years of development.

In my business we've seen four major [product] systems become obsolete in the last twelve years; we have to recover all outlay on development work within three years.

To some extent, in some fields, such as pharmaceuticals, computers, and consumer products, the strategic problems can be tackled by deciding whether to adopt a "first-in" strategy or to become "an imitator at low cost"; however, life cycles are often so short that even imitators can encounter great problems. Clearly, for the future, the important managerial competencies will hinge on the ability to operate effectively within time frames that were inconceivable a few years ago. Many organizations have become conditioned to think about developments over periods of years; in the future they may have to achieve the same results in months. This will demand a complete overhaul of attitudes, structures, and practices.

New Network Concepts of Organization

The new technology is helping to create networks among organizations. In Chapter Two, reference was made to Just-in-Time (JIT) production, which unites manufacturers, subcontractors, suppliers, and retailers in integrated systems of activity, so that goods and services are delivered to the required places a few hours before they are needed. These networks are held together by automated information systems that direct and coordinate the complete system of activities. As a result, the manufacturing firm that once saw itself as a separate enterprise now recognizes itself as only part of a complex web of interorganizational relations and must modify its managerial philosophies and systems to take this into account.

This requires that internal control be delegated to those

directly involved in work activities, and all elements of the system have to be finely tuned to meet the contingencies that arise. Given the very short time frames for coordination, information must travel as rapidly as possible to where it is needed—via computer terminals rather than through lines of command—and receive immediate attention. Self-organization among employees also becomes an important requirement. The smart firms quickly learn that it is necessary to extend the scope of their management process and take an active interest in the management practices of their suppliers and subcontractors. Given that these firms are working with just a few hours' inventory, production can be completely disrupted if suppliers fail to deliver materials on time. Therefore, before suppliers are selected, their attitudes toward management and labor and their abilities to be effective partners must be evaluated. Novel methods of introducing new production and management processes must also be developed. It is the complete network of relations—which may involve many firms—that must be managed. The development of effective interorganizational relations and mindsets that are able to sustain and develop patterns of mutual dependence become as important as the design and operation of specific activities.

JIT management systems are prototypical of a trend linked with developments in electronic technology. As well, I see a related phenomenon developing in the service sector as new firms find their success bound together with the capabilities created by the new technology. For example, the new integration among firms in different areas of the financial services industry has been made possible by the same technological developments that gave rise to JIT management. The recent decentralization of banks—which has resulted in automatic teller machines springing up in supermarkets, drugstores, shopping malls, airports, and recreation centers—provides another obvious example.

The internal restructuring of firms through the development of automated office systems—which include interacting computer terminals, electronic mail systems, data banks, facsimile transfer systems, conference-style telephones and video systems, and other related systems that replace direct physical interaction—again illustrates the emergence of the network concept. The new technology allows a physical restructuring of the organization making it more like an electronic spider's web than a pyramid. As one CEO put it:

> In principle, many of my staff needn't come to work. They can interact through computer terminals, and a completely decentralized office is possible. Technology can be used to dissolve geographical barriers. People can dialogue without being in the office. There is absolutely no reason why our organization should be located in Toronto rather than being spread out across a number of cities at the same time. We can do the same kind of work wherever we are located.

Such changes, which presently represent potential rather than reality for most firms, also demand new styles of thinking about one's organization and how it can be sustained and developed over time.

All these examples draw attention to the same point. The new technology is creating the possibility for radically new styles of organization to emerge. But these new styles demand important managerial competencies in relation to the design of information systems, managerial philosophies and mindsets, principles of integration and control (especially those relating to remote management), and the ability to create a work environment integrated by shared values and directions, even though there are very few opportunities for direct personal interaction. As the machine age produced large centralized bureaucracies, the electronic age is producing networks as the primary organizational form. Though the trend is technology driven, many of the competencies rest on the human side. As two executives with direct experience of JIT systems reported:

> The process involves a cultural change as much as a technical change. It requires new attitudes from both management and labor.

It is a people process that changes the company.

This human dimension of the high-tech, network style of management must always be kept firmly in mind.

New Modes of Work Design

Secretaries are becoming managers and many managers are becoming secretaries! As the new technology is introduced, conventional roles, patterns of decision making, and general relations change.

The new technology allows you to program so much more for influencing people lower in the organization that you can eliminate middle management. Many CEOs think that middle managers are dispensable because top managers don't need them. But the fact is that the people at the *bottom* no longer need them.

We have the potential to manage our organizations with a much smaller professional staff. The new technology allows us to reduce the number of layers in the hierarchy to get better information, to speed communications, and to make better decisions.

In my organization a shift is occurring: managers no longer just see themselves as people using the new technology. They see themselves as managers of transition—as managers of processes that never stop. Office automation does not exist as a specific phenomenon—it exists in terms of a number of different things: in the shift in focus from accounting to data-base management; from information processing to communications; and from [large-scale] work-processing systems to [smaller-scale] work stations. Several related but distinct activities are going on at the same time.

People are able to get data they could never dream about getting before. They are able to make smaller and smaller segments of the organization cost or profit centers. They are still using computers to do a lot of traditional things, like word processing, but many new things can be done as well.

One of the big impacts is the change from many independent data bases in private filing cabinets to a single base where everyone has the same information.

In my previous organization I was the vice-president in charge of development of a major product. At one time I had one hundred and four task forces reporting to me. The use of electronic mail cut six months off the process. It couldn't have been done without this method of keeping people informed and knowing what they needed to know.

These comments capture in detail some ways in which information technology is impacting organizations. Properly designed and used, the technology is capable of transforming how we think about work processes and can do much to facilitate the self-organization and remote management discussed earlier. A crucial feature of the technology rests in its ability to flatten organizational structures through the transformation of work. Hierarchical styles of management tend to separate thinking and doing, concentrating control and initiative at higher levels. The new technology has a democratizing influence, because its full benefits are realized only when all employees are encouraged to exercise full initiative in relation to their tasks.

Consider, for example, the benefits to be realized from

the introduction of electronic mail and interactive data bases. These have the capacity to change the nature of work and decision making, diffusing the distinction between managerial and operational roles. These systems allow information to be shared on an ongoing basis. People can tune in to the latest situation and offer their views at an early stage. As one CEO put it:

> I find that the system allows more collateral decision making. Informal surveys of the "What do you think?" variety tend to go on all the time, as a form of taking the pulse. People can sound out and test opinion, and modify the ideas they're working on. If you make reports and general information accessible, and have [electronic] mail slots for new ideas, a lot of people can get in on the decision. Before, they had to be specifically informed about what was happening. Now, they can get involved on their own initiative. The process opens the whole organization. You find that you have a kind of radar that you didn't have before.

The same is true of factory work. Where you bring computer terminals onto the shop floor—as part of a JIT system or as support for autonomous work groups or other team-based work systems—initiative is passed down to the operational level. The well-trained factory worker is given the opportunity to do tasks and make decisions that were once reserved for supervisors. The same is true in large offices, where the new technology is used to support comprehensive work stations staffed by teams of highly skilled people, self-organizing a wide range of tasks formerly performed by different people in assembly-line fashion.

The new technology has the potential to reshape the nature of work dramatically. But to do so, managers and systems designers must be able to break free of bureaucratic constraints. If old mindsets dominate use of the new technology, improvements and efficiencies are likely to be marginal. The real payoff seems to be the opportunity to transform work processes. Or, as one executive put it, "You have to use the technology to automate tasks and work processes, not just to automate jobs." It is necessary to step back, rethink the whole process, and see how the technology can be used to create new modes of work organization.

As is well known, one effect of the technology is elimination of many conventional jobs. A number of executives reported that information technology had been introduced in their organizations with the goals of reducing staff, cutting costs, and improving efficiency.

> You have to have the technology to keep up. It has a big impact on staffing. We now employ 750 instead of 1,000 people in one of our divisions.

> Despite all the problems with the technology, we estimate that we've been able to cut administrative costs from 29 cents to 24 cents on the dollar.

> While the most explicit reason for introducing the new technology has been to reduce staff, its effect has been to reduce new hires. There have not been many layoffs; staff has been reduced through attrition. The technology has also added flexibility, facilitating a four-day week in the recession.

At the same time, many executives argue that it is necessary to approach the new technology as part of a "leap of faith" that may lead to a qualitatively new situation. One should always look for cost savings, but should also be aware of "the opportunity side" of the cost–benefit relationship, in terms of creating a much smarter and more effective workforce, making better-quality decisions, and establishing better systems of communications, accountability, and control and better relations with suppliers and customers. As indicated in the remarks at the beginning of this section, technology has the capacity to *transform* traditional relations between management and the workforce. It has the capacity to dissolve the constraints and bound-aries that arise when people are artificially separated by rigidly defined roles. The new technology is basically an empowering technology, in the sense that it creates new opportunities for people, whether managers, production workers, clerks, or secre-taries, to exercise initiative. The real benefit of the technology is realized when it is supported by managerial mindsets that mo-bilize this initiative.

Real-Time Decision Making

Information technology can have a profound effect on decision making and accountability by bringing people into an "on-line" situation with major implications for managerial com-petencies.

The benefits of well-designed information-management systems are well known. The new technology creates an oppor-tunity to link information bases, allowing people to produce re-ports on the basis of information from many sources, to "dia-logue" with colleagues, to test out ideas against new information sources, and to zero in or control minute aspects of operations. People in different parts of an organization can become truly interconnected because of improved communications.

These are some obvious benefits of an "on-line" system of communication that must be considered in the development of competencies; however, there are other implications of being "on-line" that can exert both positive and negative effects. The situation was well summarized by one CEO in the following terms:

> The new technology makes decision making real time. Increasingly, executives have to make de-cisions now! It changes the way they do business. They can't procrastinate. They can't say they weren't in or didn't see a particular memo, because when they log into their mail system, the situation is irreversible. There is no excuse for not being to-tally current. Even when one is away from the of-

fice, there is no excuse for not logging in and collecting messages or reading the latest draft of a report.

Traditionally, many managers have learned to delay decisions to create time to maneuver. With electronic modes of communication this is difficult. When a piece of mail is read, the sender may be told "message received." When the minutes of a meeting or a copy of a report is read, the system records the event. As a result of these pressures, managers are forced to quicken their pace of work and decision making:

> The procrastinators are much more easily identified by the new technology, with twenty-four hours [to make decisions], not the usual six weeks.

Although the speeding up of communications is extremely beneficial, it is a two-edged sword. It keeps everyone informed, but at what sometimes proves to be a neck-breaking pace.

The process has many implications for managers, especially in terms of the ability to make quick decisions on specific issues while retaining the broader picture in view. It has implications for managerial accountability; managers must learn to deal with issues that they might otherwise avoid. There are also implications for the politics of decision making. As is well known, timing can be vital in the exchange of information, and the process of sending copies to crucial others is an important political art. The new technology adds new dimensions to information exchange; it speeds up and broadens communications in a positive way, but adds to the "political" complexity of the manager's role.

Small Is Beautiful

> Small is beautiful. There is something about how the new technology works that favors small units and small companies.

Small organizations are often able to get better [systems] designs, better response capacities, and less fragmentation and incompatibility. They can move in and cope with changes much more swiftly.

The incompatibility of data sets in large firms often creates chaos–different parts of the organization find that they can't "talk" to each other.

The massive players with huge projects often have huge transition problems and find themselves throwing money into a bottomless pit that keeps getting deeper.

Centralized companies depend on centralized communications. In small firms there can be more playing around. Large organizations have to hold it all together; otherwise, many separate empires develop.

Are we in a time of transition where certain firms that are able to take advantage of [new developments] will gain an edge, while others [for example, the big multinationals] will lose out?

These remarks have a consistent theme: large size is a great disadvantage. Technology is able to overcome many problems associated with large size by improving communications, but development of a coherent system to achieve this improvement can prove horrendous. Small firms often find, or develop, packaged software systems that are ideally suited to their needs; they can experiment until a good solution or design is found. Large organizations often find integration very difficult. Formerly separate "empires" clash. Designs in one area prove incompatible with those in another. The attempt to find common solutions to common problems results in incredibly complex systems designs that take ages to develop and implement. Small organizations may experience these problems too, but the problems seem more severe in large organizations.

This relationship between size and ability to get on top of the new technology is tied to a larger issue linking size and flexibility. We may be moving into an era when large size can prove a great liability. For most of the twentieth century, firms have expanded to capture economies of scale. Now, with the increasing turbulence of the environment, these economies are offset by the costs associated with reduced flexibility. On balance, there appears to be a correlation among small size, innovation, and adaptiveness. It is the small rather than the large firm that seems best equipped to innovate in response to changing environments. Even though large firms have access to more resources, the centralization and bureaucratization that often accompany size get in the way, giving small business units that are loosely linked to larger companies a distinct advantage:

> We seem to be entering a time when the little guys can come up from beneath the water and run rings around the larger companies.

The new technology adds to the range of opportunities for small companies:

> The present flux gives small, flexible operations a great chance to gain a competitive edge.

There are implications here for both large and small organizations. Small organizations must seize the opportunity and use the new technology to enhance flexibility and effectiveness. Large enterprises must use the technology to offset the drawbacks associated with size, for example, by moving toward more decentralized networks or cellular designs (see Chapter Seven). There are also many ways to modify systems design to facilitate incremental or evolutionary approaches to development, helping to make the specific problems of large-scale systems more manageable (see the section later in this chapter entitled "Open Yet Focused: Planning with Evolution in Mind").

A New Literacy

> One of the problems in introducing information technology is that highly competent people become incompetent, or feel that they are incompetent. Middle managers find change particularly difficult. They can talk about it, but they don't want to touch the keyboard. There is a barrier that must be broken.

Information technology demands a new kind of literacy based on the ability to interact through a keyboard and video. Many people find this difficult. First is the problem of typing, or "keyboard skills." Second are the problems of learning to converse with a machine and achieving a level of competence at which interaction with a computer is as comfortable as use of a telephone.

A number of the executives involved in my research project talked about the problem of computer or keyboard literacy as a key issue demanding urgent attention. Some had found solutions in in-house training programs and buddy systems, but they reported a real problem in achieving competence, particularly at a managerial level. While some managers dive right in, others encounter blocks—inability to find time, fear about incompetence and failure, the idea that typing is for secretaries or other subordinates. These problems hinge on both skills and attitudes.

Developing an adequate level of computer literacy can prove especially difficult for firms operating in interorganizational networks where staff in other organizations lag behind development. One executive described the difficulties in getting independent dealers and distributors into a mindset that would facilitate full use of the technology, even when support was provided. Here again, problems are associated with both attitudes and skills.

While many of these problems will disappear as people who have grown up in the computer age gain more influence, the issue is of critical importance in the short and medium term.

Many organizations have spent millions on computer systems that are operating at only a fraction of their potential. The computer industry has paid very little attention to the development of user skills in comparison with the development of hardware and software. A critical link in the implementation chain has thus been broken, with negative results in terms of productivity and general effectiveness. Organizations that can develop competencies in relation to computer literacy stand to gain a great deal.

New Attitudes Toward Change

Many executives maintained that successful use of the new technology is often a matter of attitude. The general climate within an organization seems to have a fundamental impact on implementation and the general responsiveness to change. In some organizations employees view change as a challenge and relish the opportunities, drive, and excitement it can create; in other organizations, change is surrounded by fear.

Naturally, discussion of the new technology usually raises very real concerns about personal competence and about employment (elimination of jobs, career opportunities, and lifestyles). These fears frequently translate into a direct resistance to change, particularly at middle management levels. According to one group of executives, fewer problems were encountered in introducing the new technology among blue-collar workers, than among white-collar workers, although this depended on the climate of labor–management relations.

If people *are* going to lose their jobs, then their fears are real and the relationship between workers and management will be strained. But in other situations, much can be done to foster a climate conducive to change. Skills training and "literacy education" can eliminate fears of incompetence and the threat posed by the unknown. Policies that avoid layoffs in favor of natural attrition or voluntary retirement can eliminate fear about job loss. Corporate philosophies committed to using the new technology to expand opportunities rather than eliminate jobs can help create a climate of genuine adventure and optimism. The new technology symbolizes challenge and opportunity, and much can be done to foster a corporate culture that rises to the occasion. Managers can do much to symbolize and communicate the key values and attitudes necessary for success, and the technology can itself be used for this purpose.

Executives who have direct experience with the technology described how it quickly becomes an important part of factory/office culture, whether as "Raymond the robot" or the "electronic grapevine" circulating the latest jokes or office gossip. The impersonal side of the technology allows employees to communicate information and concerns to managers that would be impossible to communicate face to face or in written form; it also provides managers with a means to respond speedily and clearly. This integration of the technology with daily routine can lend it a much friendlier face.

Most important, however, is the need to create an ethos that encourages employees to harness the transformative impact of the technology by finding new ways to make effective contributions to their organization. Under the old bureaucratic model of organization, roles were predefined. Under the new technology, people can define their own connections with and contributions to the whole. Indeed, the full effects of the technology can be realized only if people are prepared to use their initiative in an evolving way, changing the nature of their work as they find smarter ways of doing things. For this to occur, people must share a sense of the overall mission and values of an organization, so that they can think globally and ensure that local actions resonate with the wider objectives. The new technology has the capacity to transform organizations into "electronic villages," where people have a strong sense of interconnection and are full, active contributors to the community. Those responsible for introducing the technology must facilitate this transformation.

Open Yet Focused: Planning with Evolution in Mind

Because of the pace of technological change, the changing organizational requirements, and the evolving capacities of hardware and software, it is extremely difficult to plan for the new technology in a coherent way. Huge amounts of capital expenditure can be involved, and as often as not, there is great waste and inefficiency, especially in large-scale projects.

> There are problems in getting the perfect system; there are problems of integrating different systems and of migrating systems [from one place to another]; every [large-scale] change seems to result in a mess. There is high risk. The results are almost always a major disappointment, in that the system usually does less than you think it will. And the change almost always takes an incredible length of time. There seems to be a growing view that you should not undertake big systems change; it's generally a bad thing to do.

This view may seem rather pessimistic, but the sentiments have been echoed in many ways. The paradox is that organizations need to plan and implement the new technology with a broad picture in mind, yet they must remain free of the problems that such "big-picture planning" can generate. One must know where one is going and what one is trying to do, but avoid being trapped in plans so grand that they block speedy, effective implementation.

In practice, this paradox boils down to a choice: Should some kind of integrated design be imposed on a system, or should some broad parameters be set within which spontaneous incremental user-driven development can occur? In other words, should integration and direction be *predesigned* or allowed to *evolve?*

This issue was an important focus for some of the executives involved in my research; it lead to the general conclusion that the nature of the new technology favors focused experimentation rather than predesign. Although integrated systems are needed, it is probably much wiser to achieve this integration through processes that facilitate user collaboration and make systems designs "user driven" rather than "designer driven."

This "step-at-a-time" approach can appear as an aimless process; however, if set within the context of a clear corporate mission and with the ultimate goal in mind, this approach can allow focused yet limited steps toward a highly coherent system that avoids many of the pitfalls of centrally designed large-scale systems.

Executives, convinced of the importance of this incrementalism, discussed how it could be put into practice in terms of the following principles: line-driven change, a "step-at-a-time" projects, building around critical conditions in systems design, generating maximum user involvement, and continuous training to develop competence.

Line-Driven Change

The importance of ensuring that the contributions of specialist MIS departments serve the interests of line activities was stressed repeatedly. We have already discussed this subject in Chapter Seven with respect to making specialist staff user driven. In summary, MIS departments often approach problems in terms of their own goals, priorities, and styles of operation, seeking professionally elegant two- to five-year solution schedules, instead of the two- to five-week make-shift schedules necessary to keep abreast of current demands. The typical MIS mindset was the object of criticism, as evidenced in the following comments:

> My experience is that it's a bad policy to wait for the MIS department. They're often unhelpful. They [typically] say they can't do it, take a long time, or want to do it their way. My approach has been to go for outside help. I have driven the changes that we've introduced, avoiding MIS altogether.

> MIS departments are often trying to protect their power base, which they see as eroding. They see themselves as under threat [from the decentralization created by microcomputing] when in fact they're in an era of great opportunity. They often

try to defend the status quo, and have not made
the switch in mindset that their role demands.
They do not see that they should play the role of
troubleshooters rather than grand designers.

Hence the view that line executives should be in control of technological change, adopting a clear sponsorship role, symbolizing
the priorities and values that are to guide the implementation process, and commissioning help and advice as required. They must
embrace the change as their own and assume the same responsibility for outcomes that they hold in relation to other line activities.
To be effective in this context MIS specialists need to pay close
attention to the mindsets and competencies that allow them to
be user driven in the way they approach assignments.

"Step-at-a-Time" Projects

The integration problems posed by large-scale change led
many executives to favor bottom-up integration, achieved
through carefully designed pilot projects that attempt to surface
potential problems at an early stage. Provided such experimentation occurs within the context of a clear vision of the purposes of change and relevant priorities, it can provide the basis
for a very effective learning-oriented implementation strategy.
As one executive put it, we must replace the "no risk, no error"
mentality that often guides the work of technical specialists
with "let's see if it works and learn from our [limited] mistakes." Implementation needs to be set within a philosophy of
action-based learning.

Consistency and Integration: Critical Conditions for Systems Design

Our approach was *to avoid disasters,* such as
incompatible data sets and computers that can't
interact.

One can plan by specifying exactly what one wants, or
one can plan by specifying what one wants to avoid. The latter

approach sensitizes one to possible disasters and allows one to steer clear at an early stage. Using downside scenarios to specify the parameters of the system one would like to see in operation can create an evolutionary approach to planning that allows a greater degree of freedom for experimentation. This approach provides a means of remaining "open yet focused" toward use of the new technology.

Several critical conditions for managing the new technology are obvious:

- Consistency of computer architecture and design of data bases
- Software compatibility
- Broad and multiple points of access to data bases
- Multiple functions wherever possible
- Corporate mission and user functionality as a driving force

This list is not exhaustive. The point is that the disaster scenario methodology can be used to generate such lists for guiding decision and implementation.

Maximum User Involvement

Get the users involved in systems design as much as possible. Let them talk about what's needed.

Try to avoid seeing the project as a computer application: see it as a companywide issue that needs everyone involved.

Ask how work can be made easier and more effective and try to design systems from the front door.

Much can be done to promote integrated systems design on a piecemeal basis by adopting a philosophy of maximum user involvement in the design process. Through such means, inventory management programs sponsored by warehouse managers can be used to improve customer service as well as stock control. Accounting systems can be used to improve decision making in line departments, as well as in the controller's office. And so on. Often, systems designers overlook the multiple functions and clients a system can serve if design is viewed as an organizationwide issue. If the designer is able to broaden the ownership of a project to include other clients or stakeholders and still meet the immediate needs of the line managers who commissioned the work, then benefits will be increased and costs distributed to the advantage of all. Creating broad user involvement—on either an ad hoc or continuous basis—will go a long way to make incremental strategies systemic in their effects.

Continuous Training to Sustain Competence

Finally, there is the question of training. The best designed systems can live up to their potential only if the users are able to use them effectively. A simple point; however, numerous computers lie idle because employees have not yet developed the required level of competence or remain uninformed about the latest developments. Development and use of a computer system involve continuous learning, which can be promoted through intelligent systems design. This is particularly important if the capacity for system evolution is to be widespread.

Managing Information Overload

One of the main messages of this chapter is that the new technology demands new ways of thinking about the whole process of organization and management. Nowhere is this more evident than in the field of information management. The new technology has a capacity to generate, and provide access to, vast amounts of data, and to improve the quality of information and decision making. The design of effective information-management systems and accessible data bases can contribute much. But it is also necessary for managers and "knowledge workers" to develop appropriate mindsets and competencies that allow them to make effective use of data. Executives involved in discussing this issue identified two skills as being particularly important: the ability to sort "the wheat from the chaff"; and the ability to dialogue with data.

Sorting Wheat from Chaff

One of the main dangers of the new technology is that it can create information overload, which consumes time and clouds perceptions. In this regard, it is a two-edged sword. It can open the way to new data sources and keep people better informed, but it can also bury them in so much detail that they become paralyzed rather than empowered. It is thus essential that managers and other knowledge workers become competent at processing data, to determine what is significant and what is trivial, and develop interpretive skills that allow them to act on what they learn. Data are valuable only to the extent that they *inform* by contributing to an understanding of a situation and widen the scope for action. Thus, it is useful to distinguish between data on the one hand and information on the other. The problem lies in translating the data into significant information.

> The technological revolution is providing so much information all the time from all over the world that we are really hard-pressed to determine what is important and what is transient. The ability to pick out of this mass of stuff what we really need to look at and think about is one of the big issues facing managers these days.

> What has happened with the computer revolution is that the things that used to take so long to produce that we never got them, we now get at the drop of a hat. We've just increased the amount of public information exponentially. But we haven't really learned how to pick and choose what we really need.

> I think that businessmen feel that the more information they get, the easier the decisions are

going to be. It's not true. There is a very fundamental business value here that needs to be turned
around as far as the business community is concerned.

One of the problems with electronic mail
is that it throws a lot of garbage into the system.
Everyone "copies" everyone else on reports and
memos, producing a lot of junk mail.

The ability to sort the wheat from the chaff
is to me a crucial managerial competency. But in
many organizations, not a lot of emphasis is placed
on that skill. I don't know how you train for it.
But if you don't have this absolutely critical skill,
you make things more difficult, and I think that's
what's happening.

These views share a common theme: much attention must be
focused on the development of skills that allow us to distinguish
between data and information and to translate data into information. The ability to access significant facts, discern crucial
patterns, and draw out their implications is crucial. The computer revolution is increasing our capacity to access data, but to
be effective we have to develop greater capacities for analysis
and interpretation. As the computer age generates more data,
the problem of interpretation becomes more pressing.

This dilemma presents enormous challenges. It challenges
those involved in developing software to improve interpretive capacities electronically. It requires employees to develop new
ways of interacting with data and new approaches to decision
making. Many managers faced with the new technology maintain their old styles of decision making and information chan-
neling instead of rethinking what decisions need to be made and
how and where to make them. They become so preoccupied
with the overwhelming quantity of data that "they don't see
what's really going on."

The new technology has produced many success stories.

Many organizations have achieved spectacular results by connecting people and data and thus improving communications, decision making, and general effectiveness. Yet the success lies as much in the managerial mindsets through which the technology is used as in the technology itself. Considerable attention must be devoted to understanding and developing the philosophies and specific competencies that will cultivate these mindsets.

Dialogue and Information Management

> With the new technology you have to find out a lot of things as you go along, by asking questions as to whether you are using it right.

Earlier we discussed whether information technology should be implemented through a grand design or incrementally. This issue formed part of a wider discussion suggesting that there are close parallels between having a conversation and using the new technology. Whether a new computer is being introduced or a person is learning to use a computer terminal or new software or to interact with a data base, the learning is accomplished through dialogue. This ability to converse in an open-minded, inquiring manner is a very important competency in effective use of the new technology.

Very often, managers look for recipes that solve their problems with one stroke. Sometimes this works. But, more often, the search for overarching designs must be tempered with an element of learning by doing. As soon as a solution to one problem is found, another problem arises. The pace and nature of change in information technology consistently throws things out of alignment, even when solutions fitting immediate needs exist. The ability to engage in a learning-oriented "conversation" with the situation seems to be a critical aspect of the mindset required to use the new technology effectively, whether in designing or using a particular computer system or in accessing a data bank. Recipes may be useful as starting points, but in times of change, effective dialogue and learning are the real keys to information management.

The Strategic Role of Software

Organizations must have good software to realize the full benefits of information technology; however, in the view of some executives, software is the neglected side of computer development. Much of the glamour and excitement lies on the hardware side of the business, leaving software in the shadow. Or, if we return to the airplane analogy at the beginning of this chapter, while hardware development is traveling 600 mph at an altitude of 35,000 feet, the weak links in implementation leave computer users struggling on the ground.

According to an old golfing adage, one "drives for show; putts for dough." The same principle applies to the relationship between hardware and software. Hardware creates the potential to achieve marvelous results, but it is the effective use of software that delivers the results. This creates special challenges for organizations in commissioning or developing software that will keep them at the cutting edge of developments and for the software industry in general.

It is difficult to overemphasize the strategic importance of the software industry in the information age. For in many organizations, the key to effectiveness rests in the hands of software firms. This has great importance for industrial strategy on a national level, because it defines one of the critical means by which a nation can develop or lose a competitive edge. In the 1970s the Japanese demonstrated how to create breakthroughs within the framework of established industries by focusing on neglected areas of development. For the 1980s and 1990s the software industry seems to define a similar realm of opportunity within the computer industry. The real payoffs within the industry may not rest in keeping at the cutting edge of technological development, but in focusing on how developments can be used effectively. Instead of being overly concerned with riding on the plane, many organizations may achieve success by focusing on the links between those on the plane and those on the ground.

A case is easily made for the strategic significance of software development and implementation. But in the view of executives who discussed this issue, there is another argument: the development of many cutting-edge managerial competencies are being delegated to the computer industry by default!

> The responsibility for implementing many new developments, such as JIT management, is being pushed back onto the software industry. Organizations are going to software firms [or internally to MIS departments] and saying "do this for us." In effect, they want the software industry to take them into the future.

The significance is obvious: the responsibility for implementing cutting-edge developments is in many cases being delegated to groups that may have no special knowledge of the tasks thrust upon them. Usually, software people are interested mainly in computers, not management. Although the best firms attempt to bridge this gulf, in many areas of the software industry, the division is real.

> The software industry often does not have the skills and expertise necessary to make a full contribution. Often, people learn about developments in management second-hand. There needs to be real top-level management insight, knowledge, and expertise [within the industry], and at all levels, both in terms of established people and new recruits.

As business and administrative systems and the needs of their users grow more sophisticated, programmers and systems designers will need to become increasingly sophisticated in their knowledge of user requirements and potential problems. At a minimum this requires that urgent attention be given to management education in the software industry, and to uniting the knowledge and experience of managers and software people. Given the key strategic role of the software industry in making JIT and other cutting-edge developments in management a reality, this critical issue may mean the difference between break-down and breakthrough.

There are implications and opportunities here for at least three groups. First, those in the business of producing packaged or customized software must develop managerial knowledge, managerial abilities, and user orientation—keys to product development and customer service. The more easily firms can adopt a user orientation, allowing them to become fully involved in both development and use of software in a managerial context, the better the overall product.

Second, software users must be aware of the potential pitfalls in delegating key developments to the software industry and must be sure to recognize and minimize the effects of knowledge gaps.

Third, there are enormous opportunities for those in the field of management education. The software industry not only represents an important niche; it could prove to be *the* critical niche in influencing the development and diffusion of cutting-edge managerial competencies in a more general sense.

9

Managing Complexity and Ambiguity

It's so simple—if you only know how!

This message is expressed in many different ways in all the "hot" books on modern management. Famous managers and consultants seem to be unanimous in stressing the importance of simple managerial principles as a basis for success.

The executives involved in my research project seemed more skeptical. Although it was recognized that an organization can derive enormous benefit from doing basic things well, complexity rather than simplicity seems to define the character of the managerial game. Wherever they look, managers are confronted with complexity. Situations are shaped by multiple stakeholders with multiple understandings, multiple expectations, and multiple demands. These situations are often ambiguous and paradoxical. They demand that managers attend to many aspects at one time. The idea that these situations are basically very simple may be appealing, but the stark reality is that they are very complex.

Presently, the major task facing many managers seems to be that of managing complexity. It is often necessary to find simple ways of cutting through the complexity, for example, by developing visions that unite diverse stakeholders, by creating market orientations that focus on important components of the external environment, by attending to the needs of employees to develop human potential. Yet, there is real danger in dwelling on the myth of simplicity. It is more realistic to accept complexity as a basic feature of modern reality and fine tune our "antennae" to interpret this complexity so that it is more manageable.

We have already begun to address this task and have pointed to numerous ways in which managers can tackle the complexity of changing environments, the challenges of the new information age, the problems of blending creativity and discipline and of reconciling the needs of today and tomorrow, and so on. All the emerging competencies that we have discussed are relevant to this endeavor.

The purpose of this chapter, therefore, is to place the reality of complexity firmly in view and highlight some of its key dimensions. For as one executive stated, "the management of complexity is something that is likely to be with us permanently. It's not going to get less and less."

I focus on three aspects of this complexity:

- Managing multiple stakeholders
- Managing many things at once
- Managing transition

Together, these profile the managerial problems that are likely to increase in importance in the years ahead.

Managing Multiple Stakeholders

Three parallel trends are reshaping the nature and pattern of managerial responsibility and accountability in a profound manner: the shift from a *shareholder* to a *stakeholder* concept of organization, the shift from *discrete organizations* to *networks,* and the shift from *highly integrated* businesses to *potpourri* collections of highly differentiated units. Each of these trends creates its own set of problems and challenges.

A Stakeholder Concept of Organization

Stakeholder power is becoming as important as shareholder power. The flux in social values makes it increasingly important for managers to realize their multiple responsibilities to a wide group of stakeholders that may include employees, customers, distributors, the community, politicians, and special interest groups, as well as owners or shareholders. Increasingly, organizations are influenced and "run" by these stakeholders to such an extent that traditional lines of responsibility are becoming increasingly difficult to discharge. Different stakeholders tend to put their interests at the forefront of organizational activities, making the task of management a very difficult balancing act. The interests of shareholders have to be balanced against those of employees, and the interests of both these groups must be reconciled with customer satisfaction. Policies advancing the interests of an organization must be balanced with those of the local community or of active interest groups. And so on. Although shareholders hold ultimate power over managers with respect to hiring and firing and demand that their interests be first, successful long-term management always involves the simultaneous management of multiple interests.

This is a very real problem for many managers, especially chief executives, and for society at large. The problems of excessive union power have already attracted much public attention. In the view of some executives, abuse of shareholder power is also becoming of great concern. For example, as one CEO put it:

> Many large institutional shareholders are interested primarily in immediate returns, not long-term gains. [This has] already caused a debasement in our consumer products business, when there is no rationale whatsoever, except short-term expectations.

The point is intended to be no more than illustrative. Excessive demands, whether they come from shareholders, unions, community groups, or politicians, can have major negative impacts on an organization. Managers must deal with these impacts in a power-loaded context, where they often feel as if they are peering down the barrel of a gun. Somehow or other, they must work toward a more favorable situation that allows them the freedom to be effective. Here are some ideas: recognize the "stake" and potential contributions of stakeholder groups, adopt stakeholder perspectives in the planning process, and develop stakeholder concepts of accountability.

Recognizing Stakeholder Groups. Corporate philosophies that recognize and emphasize the role and potential contributions of different stakeholders should be adopted. One executive reported that his organization was systematically moving toward an explicit concept of "a multistakeholder business controlled by investors, employees, managers, and customers." Another executive reported his desire to inspire shareholders and employees to recognize the importance of customer power as a critical force.

> The customer is king. The customer is really in [in our industry] now . . . and our employees and shareholders don't really understand that. We need to change this attitude.

By recognizing and confronting the diverse interests that shape an organization, and by building initiatives that bind those interests together, it is possible to create new relationships among stakeholders as attitudes, understanding, and general involvement are transformed.

Stakeholders and the Planning Process. Involvement of critical stakeholders in the planning process (even if only solicited for feedback) is also critical. Very often, organizations attempt to simplify the planning process by eliminating the influence of potentially disruptive elements. That influence, of course, is usually delayed rather than removed, because it surfaces later as opposition to implementation:

> If you elicit real feedback from your stakeholders, by God, it gives you a pile of garbage to deal with [but you can learn a great deal]. We have been trying to debate in our organization who is more important . . . customers, shareholders, staff?

If you can somehow get your people to understand what it is like being an owner, as well as just being an employee [it can make a great deal of difference].

Stakeholder Accountability. The very nature of the stakeholder concept of organization carries with it a pluralistic view of accountability. Managers that feel accountable to their staff, their customers, their community, and their shareholders will approach their responsibilities in a much more sophisticated manner than they would in situations where authority and responsibility flow to and from a single source. The manager of the future will need to be a good negotiator, at times a great statesman, capable of finding the unifying themes that allow fundamental conflicts between stakeholders to be resolved.

From Discrete Organizations to Networks

Another aspect of the changing pattern of stakeholder relations is found in the network concept of organization. The idea of a discrete organization with identifiable boundaries (whether defined in terms of physical location, the manufacturing process, or staff employed) is breaking down. Under the influence of microelectronics, JIT management, and various subcontracting arrangements, organizations are becoming more amorphous networks of interdependent organizations where no element is in firm control. Even though such a network may have a powerful focal organization, for example, a large manufacturer surrounded by a constellation of independent JIT suppliers and distributors, the focal organization is as dependent as the other organizations in the network. Interdependence is the key. Gone is the old-fashioned notion of a hierarchy in which one member (for example, the focal organization) directs the activities of other members. In comes the notion of a network that must be managed as a system of interdependent stakeholders.

This network management is fostered by a new sense of collective identity, managerial philosophies that recognize the importance of mutual dependence and collaboration and a collective sense of accountability and control. Whereas in a world of discrete organizations accountability and control tend to be oriented *inward*, in network structures they must also be oriented *outward*. Whereas under the discrete system control was often exercised unilaterally, for example, as directives from a chief executive, in the network system, control has to be more consensual. Control in a network rests in the *management of relations* rather than in the management of discrete activities. Interorganizational relations become as important as intraorganizational relations, and need to be developed at many levels. Managers must become orchestrators, negotiators, and experts in "reading" and "nudging" situations in the appropriate direction. The ability to develop mechanisms that promote mutual influence becomes more important than the ability to dominate. In complex systems, control always rests in the system of relations *between* important actors, rather than in the power of individuals. Informal alliances and shared understanding, as well as more formalized means of interaction and exchange, become critical. The core philosophy was well expressed by one chief executive:

> In the modern world you have to get alliances in many ways, whether it's alliances with other manufacturers or distributors, or simply with other managers who are trying to do the same thing. If we in Canada are going to succeed, we have to help each other out.

The ability to recognize patterns of interdependence and achieve collaboration between diverse stakeholders lies at the heart of network management. It is this appreciation of the interests that can unite and mobilize a diversified network that leads to a shared vision.

From High Integration to Potpourri

A third trend impacting stakeholder management is the emergence of potpourri forms of organization, where diverse businesses are brought under a single umbrella of control. Many executives had serious reservations about this development, because often there is no clear rationale behind patterns of acquisition. Although some organizations have clear strategies of diversification in "buying into other business," others seem to jump on the bandwagon or "desire growth for growth's sake."

It is clear how this trend adds to the scale and difficulty of stakeholder management. It is difficult enough to manage the various stakeholders in a single highly integrated business; however, in a conglomerate, the complications are multiplied: each business has its own set of stakeholders, its own corporate culture, and, often, its own distinctive style of management. The complexity of the problem is impacted by the degree of integration demanded by the parent organization. To the extent that stakeholder management at the local level can be delegated through remote management (discussed in Chapter Seven), the problem can be eased. But where integration is sought, difficulties often arise. To integrate one organization with another requires a great deal of blending:

> Blending is key . . . it is absolutely essential for everyone to have a sense of why you're in business, and where everything fits. You have to blend people, you have to blend organizations, and you have to blend cultures. [If you're not sensitive to this] you shear and cut off so much in the reorganization process.

The problem raises a paradox, because strategic acquisitions often call for some measure of integration. Although some businesses can be acquired and justifiably "left alone," acquisitions are often pursued because they do something for core activities. As one chief executive put it:

> The strategic links with the core businesses are critical. You have to be doing something through your acquisitions or it just ends up as low-quality growth . . . growth for growth's sake.

Close attention must be paid to blending skills, particularly as they relate to stakeholder management, as it is the stakeholders that ultimately must be blended.

Managing Many Things at Once

Every manager knows the problem. More tasks must be completed than time allows. Thus, management hinges on prioritizing, the ability to decide what is truly important. Managers must develop the capacity to coordinate many tasks simultaneously, yet avoid managing too many tasks. This skill is an important managerial competency and is likely to become critical as the pace and diversity of organizational life increase. Here, we focus on three aspects of this skill.

Being Excellent in Every Way

Whatever the task, it should be done to the best of one's ability, at both the individual and the corporate level. Organizations often focus on employing highly specialized staff and in gaining a competitive advantage in a single area—production, marketing, distribution, customer service. In the past, this tactic has often provided the recipe for success. Nevertheless, according to a number of executives, the demands of the modern world are such that many organizations and their employees have to broaden the basis of their competence to achieve excellence in different dimensions:

> As I see the future for manufacturing companies . . . I don't care what the books say, you have to be excellent in every way, whether it's manufacturing, whether it's distribution, whether it's organization, finance, or whatever. You've got to be good everywhere because this is a very competitive world.

This comment refers to manufacturing, but is applicable elsewhere as well. Broad-based competence is at a premium in every sector of the economy. Increasingly, managers will need to learn the art of raising and balancing standards of performance in different areas to ensure that their staff achieve excellence in "the five or six things that really count," rather than being superb in just one. At the same time, they have to avoid the trap of mediocrity.

Getting Beyond Either–Or

So often, we think in terms of dichotomies—either this *or* that. Sometimes, such choices must be made, but in the future, a premium will be placed on transcending dichotomies to find ways in which opposing forces can be combined. This topic has been discussed previously, for example, the need to combine excellence on many dimensions at once, to fuse creativity and discipline, to blend the interests of today and tomorrow, to combine "hard" finite analytical skills with "softer" intuitive ones. Leadership and participation are often considered opposing principles, whereas in fact they can and often need to be combined. Although winning is counterposed with losing, situations can often be made win–win.

Managers will need to deal with this paradox and to develop the attitudes and imagination that allow them to fuse or transcend potentially opposing requirements. They will have to frame problems so that new understandings and solutions emerge. They will have to think in terms of degree—how much of this or that rather than all of this or all of that. The skill of managing many things at once often requires that we learn to move on many fronts simultaneously.

Managing Multiple Meanings

Even the simplest situation can mean different things to different people. Though it seems simple, it is often complex. Consider, for example, a situation in which two employees are in conflict. The situation can be resolved simply enough through a unilateral action—"we'll do it this way!" But, underlying the conflict may be a variety of competing ideas, facts, and interpretations that may make perfect sense to the holder but are contradictory to the rival. Effective management of such situations ultimately depends on the ability to understand many dimensions simultaneously, to provide the basis for creative rather than dogmatic responses. The importance of this skill to managerial competence is clear when we realize that the conflict just described is often found on a larger scale in interdepartmental, interorganizational, and intersectoral (for example, business-government) relations.

Managing Transition

Another important aspect of modern complexity is the state of flux that seems to be the order of the day:

Products seem to have shorter and shorter life cycles.
Technology changes at an increasingly rapid pace.
Skills become obsolete faster.
Information and knowledge are subject to continuous transformation.

A number of executives wondered whether high rates of change are here to stay or whether we are in a particularly difficult period:

Is the present situation akin to rapids on a river? Will we come out of the rapids with different organizational structures and managerial processes that will make everything a little easier?

Opinion leaned toward the idea that a major restructuring is under way; however, whether the pace and nature of change will slow down is an open question. Flexibility and adaptiveness are likely to continue to be at a premium, and managers are well advised to consider management of complex change as a basic competency for the years ahead.

Good managers need to develop a capacity to deal with uncertainty and ambiguity at a fast

speed, . . . and to develop effective ways of handling
large amounts of information and complex issues.
Some people get paralyzed; others keep going. This
ability to overcome paralysis is a real competency.

To cope with change, and to manage complexity in general, an open, learning-oriented stance is essential. Managers
must be able "to go with the flow" and must recognize that
learning is an essential, continuous part of the process. Where
change and complexity dominate, there is no substitute for
learning. In the future this attitude must be made central to the
corporate philosophy through which organizations approach the
challenges posed by complex change.

10

Broadening Competencies
and Reframing Contexts

෨෨෨ Worldwide, organizations seem to be surrounded by interlocking problems rooted in the very nature of economic and social life. These problems vary from country to country, and are usually perceived in different ways. They are most often expressed as a national malaise: sluggish economic growth, persistent unemployment, lack of competitive flair, stifling government regulation, lackluster management, poor industrial relations, unequal patterns of social and regional development, poor economic location, and so on. This theme emerged with incredible force throughout my research. Time and again, discussion and analysis of the problems and challenges facing specific organizations turned into a discussion and analysis of the problems and challenges facing Canadian organizations in general.

The most popular launch pad for this discussion was the idea that many Canadian organizations are in a "weak competitive position" in relation to their neighbors in the United States and in relation to the new competition emerging with "globalization" of the world economy. As the contributory factors were explored, numerous related issues were brought into play: such as concerns about the "Canadian psyche," "high levels of social expenditure and social expectations," the potential for "a growing polarization in society," poor labor–management relations, problems with government regulation, absence of "effective political leadership," absence of "a sense of vision for Canada," and dissatisfaction with the educational system.

Discussion was often characterized by deep divisions over

values and opinions relating to the significance of the problems and what could or should be done. No real consensus emerged; however, the discussion did highlight a crucial point: if Canadian organizations are truly interested in developing managerial competencies that will enable them to be effective in the global economy, they will have to pay attention to the problems shaping the context in which they are operating. In addition to managing relations within their organizations and with their closest stakeholders, they will have to develop an appreciation for, and skill in influencing, broader contextual issues.

In this chapter, we discuss these "contextual competencies." We build on an analysis of problems associated with executives' perceptions of Canada's relatively weak position in the world economy; however, the basic ideas have international application. Though other countries may not face exactly the same problems Canada does, the fates of their organizations are still shaped by parallel dynamics. Non-Canadian readers should thus try to understand how problems associated with Canada's weak competitive position, national psyche, business–government relations, and so on, are equivalent to problems faced by their own countries, even though character, strengths, and weaknesses may differ. These readers should try to use the Canadian situation, and the ideas and responses of the Canadian executives, as a springboard for developing appropriate "contextual competencies" in their own countries.

National Influences on Canada's Competitive Position

If you look at Canadian history, it has been a strong, rich country, never innovative, never upset, a very peaceful people, people with a willingness to absorb and accept the mosaic [of] different cultures that were coming in. It has been a rich, fat, happy nation. But today, we are living in a different world: a world where our resources will no longer carry us, a world where our government is spending more than it takes in, which eventually . . . will lead to trouble. We are faced with a crisis of competition, to which we have to react . . . and

we have got to react now, because if we don't react, our standard of living will . . . decline.

If the Canadian dollar weren't so low, a lot
of organizations would just close down.

There are success stories. Many Canadian organizations
are doing extremely well. But, as suggested above, there are real
problems.

Figure 6 illustrates the thrust of discussions on this issue.
The problems facing Canadian organizations were viewed as
complex and wide-ranging. Today, the problem of Canadian
competitiveness is frequently tied to the issue of "free trade"
with the United States. Although the majority of executives favored freer trade, they also recognized that Canadian organizations must improve their competitive ability to meet the challenges that more open arrangements would bring. Regardless of
the decision on free trade, it is important that Canadian organizations use this opportunity to assess their strengths and weaknesses, with the goal of improving their position. As one CEO
stated:

I think the free trade debate is extremely
helpful, [because] it is forcing every player in the
Canadian economy, including labor, to look at
themselves in terms of the world stage, in terms of
their relative competitiveness. And if it does nothing else but sharpen all of us . . . [it will be] a major contribution.

In the following pages, I highlight those areas of particular concern in assessing Canada's competitive position, and indicate policy issues that require consideration in developing competitive ability at a national level.

Canada: A Resource-Based Economy in Decline?

The following theme was restated in many ways: Canada
has the mindset of a resource-rich nation, but has not come to

Figure 6. Weaknesses in Canada's Competitive Position:
A Synopsis of Executive Opinions.

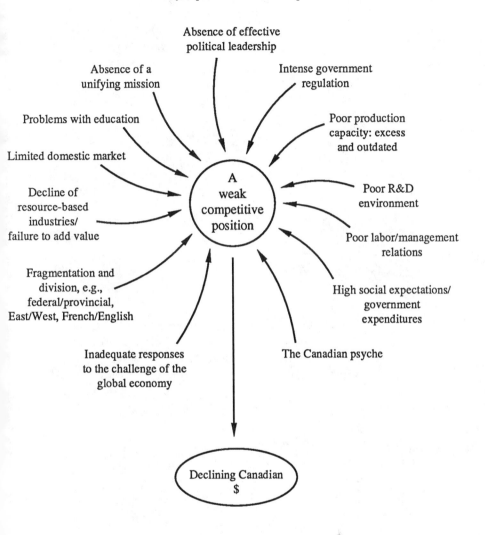

"We're standing on quicksand."

"Come hell or high water, we've got to export . . . the world
will force us to do it—by pushing our exchange rate down
to the place where we cannot consume so much ourselves."

grips with the fact that its natural resources are almost spent
and that a new orientation toward socioeconomics is necessary.
As one CEO put it:

> In the past we've had a tendency to "milk
> the cow." We have chopped down the trees and
> used our resources. Now we need to give much
> more attention to the problem of creating value.
> We have to find ways of being more creative and of
> rising to the challenges that lie ahead.

Other executives talked about how governments and other institutions have "amortized" or "disguised" underlying
problems through various economic adjustments. Because Canada has been resource-rich, social expectations are extremely
high, and excellent "safety nets" and social programs have developed. The high standards have been sustained through increases in government expenditure and indebtedness, high levels
of taxation, and the falling Canadian dollar; these disguise the
fundamental economic adjustments that are taking place. The
net result, in the view of at least one executive, is that "Our resource advantage has now levered us into a poor position. We
have a better standard of living then we deserve."

The forecast for the future is one of atrophy or crisis
(these scenarios are discussed later), unless Canada can continue
to find new means of creating the wealth once provided by
natural resources. The consensus is that the future prosperity of
Canada rests in the skills of its people, rather than in the ground.
These skills must be nurtured so that they will "add value" to
the products of traditional industries and within the context of
the new services and industries that are emerging as part of Canada's transition to the high-tech, "information age."

Intense Government Regulation

In addition to the problems created by high levels of government expenditure and taxation, which add to the cost of
doing business in Canada, the "intense level" of government

regulation was cited as a major barrier to competitiveness. Note the following complaints.

> *Unrealistic Requirements:* "Insist that in addition to spending $10 million to remove 99% of a problem we must go all the way and spend another $10 million to remove the remaining 1%."
>
> *Excessive Restrictions:* "We are highly restricted in what we can do, no matter where we do it. We have to get permission . . . to make changes in the business we conduct in Hong Kong, Houston, or wherever. And that is a major constraint."
>
> *Outdated Regulations:* "The major legislation [influencing our industry] changes about once every ten years . . . and that isn't quite rapid enough to keep things moving along these days."
>
> *Fragmented Regulations:* "One of the problems is that governments rarely look at problems as wholes. Attention is split to fit the interests of different departments that respond to the problem on the basis of their own limited interests. The result is that you get a series of separate sets of regulations, each of which has a rationale and makes sense in a limited way, but doesn't make sense overall."
>
> *Absence of Universal Standards:* "Why can't joint standards be worked out between Canada and the United States? The differences are stifling."
>
> *Absence of "Due Process":* "In Canada, there is no way of bringing a bureaucrat to a decision, thereby forcing the pace. In the United States, if you disagree with a regulator you can set up a tribunal to investigate. Since there is no way [in Canada] of taking on a bureaucrat so that he comes to grips with an issue, you tend to do as you're told. They sit on projects and you have to wait interminably. In the United States everything is so much faster. The regulatory blocks are so great [in Can-

ada]. Often, you can't do interesting work because
of the blocks."

Rigid Attitudes: "In dealing with government there's always the problem of how much one
can bend the rules. The bureaucrats tend to think
in idealistic rather than practical terms. Two or
three times a day you find yourself asking: How
far can I take this in line with the agreed objective
[of the legislation]?"

Vagaries of Interpretation: "Regulation often
hinges on bureaucratic attitudes, rather than on the
regulations per se. And interpretations can change
in an adverse way [even if the regulations do not
change]."

Poor Labor–Management Relations

Labor–management relations were identified as a factor
critical to Canada's competitive position. It was recognized that
relations are often poor, and the blame was seen to reside in
both labor and management.

Organizations often get the union they deserve. Attempts at communication are often very
poor and breed mistrust.

The whole productivity question is a managerial problem, not a labor problem. Management
makes labor productive. I think most people want
to work hard and do a good job. And the question
is, as society changes, how do we make it easier for
that to happen?

While critical of the past, many executives were optimistic about the future. They believed the introduction of new
technology would transform power relations, putting unions in
a weaker position and making it possible for management to
achieve a better work climate through more direct communication with the workforce. Much of the present atmosphere is

based on "fear of job loss," which was seen as an opportunity to set a climate (a) for new collaborative relations in which "fight" is no longer the best strategy and (b) for elimination of work practices "that don't add value."

- Leadership qualities in managers at plant levels
- Negotiation skills
- Ability to communicate and to impact corporate culture positively
- Ability to recognize that many labor-management problems exist at a community level and must be addressed at this level if they are to be resolved

These factors were seen as important in creating the new climate. Interestingly, less optimism was expressed with respect to problems among white-collar staff:

> The resistance of blue-collar staff is much overstated; the main resistance to change is at middle management levels.

The transformations occurring in many organizations are creating much stress and insecurity among middle managers who once saw themselves as very secure. Their resistance to change is often much more difficult to detect, but can have a major impact on an organization's competitive position.

The Canadian Psyche

> It's the Canadian mindset that we have to get at. We paralyze ourselves. Outsiders would rank us much higher than we would rank ourselves. We always see the impediments. There's [a] myth that suggests we are insecure, intimidated, jealous of the United States—and it all becomes true.

> We need to think about Canada in a different way. There is a hell of a lot of creative capacity in this country.

This country has always been a country of employees, as opposed to employers. The Americans are different. I feel that we are always waiting for somebody else to tell us where to go, rather than sitting down and saying, "What is it we have to do in our own neck of the woods?"

The increasing internationalization [of world business] is going to require a very different outlook on the part of Canadians, in whatever business they are. We are [going to have] to learn how to [operate] in China, in the United States, in Nigeria, and other countries, and it's going to require a much wider understanding of cultural differences, languages, and other things. We have been a very insular people. I think that within the last twenty years, we've been as insular as the Americans were in the 1930s.

There's a story about an American kid and a Canadian kid. They're told that there's a surprise waiting for them in the room behind the closed door. When they open the door they find that the room is full of horse manure. The Canadian boy starts crying. The American boy dives in, digging as fast as he can, shouting excitedly: "With all this manure there must be a pony in here!"

We probably have one of the best safety nets, in the economic sense, in the world, and still we are unwilling to take risks.

Capital is not scarce; it's scared.

The national bird is the grouse.

These rather unflattering remarks illustrate a theme that ran throughout discussions about Canada's weak competitive position. It was emphasized that Canadians tend to be:

- Cautious and insecure
- Followers rather than leaders
- Uncertain of their identity and place in the world
- Self-denigrating
- Negative in attitude, seeing impediments rather than opportunities
- Insular in outlook
- Suffering from a "branch plant mentality"

This negativism and general lack of self-confidence were seen as crippling in terms of the ability of Canadians to be competitive. It seems that living next door to a large, rich, successful, and powerful neighbor, on one hand, and under the distant eye of a colonial parent, on the other hand, has influenced the Canadian psyche adversely. Like it or not, Canadians in general do not have a good self-image and do not live up to their potential to be a truly great socioeconomic force. Thus in the view of many executives, if Canada is to be successful in the modern world, something must be done to transform this situation.

Absence of Effective Political Leadership

These problems were also viewed as an important influence in Canadian politics. Politicians, and government in general, were seen as part of the problem underlying Canada's weak competitive position; there was only a glimmer of hope that they would become part of the solution.

I don't believe that there is any such thing as government anymore. [We have] political parties vying for power in the next election . . . and that is why we have such deficits. No one is actually asking what is good for the country. They ask what is good for our party. What will happen in the next election?

You have crazy social policy in Canada. All the politicians are looking for votes. You can't get any united action. There is no leadership in place.

There is no breakthrough in the government mind-set for solving social problems.

> I think we are spending ourselves to death. Politicians brag because they have managed to reduce the *rate of increase* of our deficit! We are moving away from the kind of percentage of GNP in our deficit that is livable. And I really think that expectations are going to have to change. If they don't, the burden business will have to carry, for example, in terms of taxation and benefits for employees, is going to be such that Canada will never benefit, with or without free trade.

Many problems were associated with the short-term horizons that shape electoral politics and the fact that political leaders are often not prepared to stand up and lead.

Absence of Vision (Mission)

> We're missing a set of unifying causes in Canada; there is no sense of national vision; everyone is fragmented. Someone has to stand up and do something about it. Federal–provincial relations are a particular problem: It's difficult to get a national stand on important issues. For example, people are not prepared to give up their privileges. We don't have a sense of purpose. We're Balkanized!

> There is a key role for the media to play in fostering knowledge and identity. At present it functions in a way that fosters division. It often misses the strategic significance of things. It does not really present the problems; it adds to the problems. The media *finds* controversy: the bleeding parts get all the press. [But, there] is a role to be played in building Canadian strengths.

Canada and Canadian politics are fragmented. Deep divisions exist between East and West, between federal and provincial levels of government, and between English- and French-speaking people. These divisions overlie a mosaic of cultural heterogeneity that adds further fragmentation.

Many executives noted how such divisions create problems for the internal administration of their organizations and also for mobilization of the national vision (mission). Although some executives questioned the viability of developing a vision or mission to which twenty-five million Canadians could subscribe, others thought it was a high priority in solving the many difficulties described above. The following exchange illustrates this division:

> A: I don't think we can define a national vision as clearly as we can define a vision within our companies. I don't think it is possible or practical, or even acceptable, to have a precise definition of where the country is going.
>
> B: I would disagree. I think each one of us in this room would be a hell of a lot more effective if we at least had a concept of what the country ought to work toward. [At the moment] nobody is talking about it. There is an absolute vagueness that feeds on politicization and a lack of government at every level in our society. I think it would be a lot more constructive . . . to have some kind of vision. I think we would be stronger.

Opinion tended to favor the latter view, emphasizing the importance of trying to find a thrust that will allow Canada to be proactive in shaping its destiny in the modern world:

> The original vision was to exploit resources and create a better life style. We now need a vision to suit our new circumstances.

> We have to make up our minds in Canada. Do we want to be a key player in the new emerging world economy, or do we want to be a raw resource

provider, a support player, a "bit" player? If Canada as a whole doesn't have a sense of its destiny,
of what part it wants to play in the world . . . [it]
will never play out its opportunity and capacity. I
feel that this is the problem with the country right
now. Even with all the diversity and differences, I
think the country is crying out for somebody, or
some group of people, to show some leadership.

Problems with Education

In the most general sense the Canadian educational system was seen as falling below the levels necessary to give Canada
a competitive edge in the world economy. At a time when the
nation should be investing in people as its most valuable resource and fostering skills that will carry it into a new stage of
development, resources are being squeezed and stretched in all
sorts of ways. Education is simply *not* a national priority.

The case was most forcibly made by executives from the
university sector, who indicated that the system was being
"starved of resources" while being stretched to meet the demands of increasing numbers of students. Although the overall
productivity of the system is up, it has been achieved in many
instances at the expense of quality and, in particular, the system's ability to produce first-class leaders—in business, chemis-
try, engineering, physics, and other disciplines crucial to Canada's future.

The products of the university system were also criticized
for being overspecialized, too theoretical, detached from the
real world, and lacking in creative ability:

> In the software industry we need people that
> can apply their knowledge. The typical computer
> science graduate can handle five or six computer
> languages, but knows *nothing* about elementary
> business systems at a practical level.

> Where are the bright kids? We used to attract
> them in consumer goods marketing. But there seems

to be a problem with [the educational] system:
they've become bright automatons.

Great concern was expressed about the high dropout rates
and the amount of illiteracy and passivity. Although these problems were seen as international in scope and as part of a general
social problem, they were also seen as critical to Canada's ability to operate as a highly developed nation. The following comment by a chief executive from the voluntary sector captures
the essence of this concern:

> We have kids coming out of public and high
> school systems that are semiliterate, and have very
> few skills to offer to the marketplace that make
> them potentially employable. So there are some
> things that have got to change in our educational
> system. There are a whole series of things that have
> to change. We need [more] literacy campaigns,
> adult education, and continuing education. Volun-
> tary organizations, community colleges, university
> extensions . . . everybody has got to work at it to-
> gether.

Challenge of Globalization

There are some Canadian organizations that are having a
real impact on the world economy. They have taken on the best
competition the world has to offer and excelled in diverse markets as widespread as Asia, Australia, Europe, Japan, and the
United States. Nevertheless, the majority have been more intro-
verted. The factors discussed earlier, as well as the fact that
many organizations are "branch plants" or are dominated by a
"branch plant mentality," confine them to a local view and limited aspirations. This was perceived as a real problem, particularly in the present view of the world as an integrated economy.
Traditional trade relations are in flux. The locus for future development has shifted away from the Atlantic connection with
Europe to the Pacific connection with the Far East. Manufacturing nations with low wage rates, such as Korea, are making

important inroads into areas of production that have long been dominated by the West. In addition, products and standards of performance are becoming internationalized. Anything that is portable, whether knowledge, a skill, a service, or a material good, now has a world market. International standards govern performance in service industries such as finance, and there are often clear expectations of what is a "quality" service or product: industry leaders now tend to set world standards. Given these developments, it is unrealistic to think of the national economy as a separate entity. National economies are parts of an integrated world economy, over which the industrial nations now have limited control.

It was felt that Canada has no option but to look outside, to become more competitive, and to rise to the challenge of new trade relations in a positive manner:

> If our response to increasing international-
> ization is *not* to go out into the world and com-
> pete, but to withdraw further, then . . . we will be-
> come less and less competitive, and the exchange
> rate will fall further, and our standard of living will
> fall, because we have such a level of external debt—
> we are not quite in the state of some of the Third
> World countries, but we are getting damn close—
> that come hell or high water, we've got to export.
> And if we do not do it willingly, the world will
> force us to [do it] —by pushing our exchange rate
> down to where we cannot afford to consume so
> much ourselves, and will *have* to export more and
> more. This has consequences for all industries. We
> have no choice . . . we either do it [now] or we
> will be forced to do it later.

Executives from organizations that are heavily involved in the international scene reported that they found it easier to do business outside Canada than they had expected, although great commitment and effort were required. The limited size of the domestic market is a constraint on development; however, by looking first to the United States and then beyond, it may be possible to expand business horizons and internationalize many Canadian organizations. Many executives feel that Canada has the strength and ability to take on the challenge, but it must be supported by national policies. For example, government could do much to "sell" Canada to U.S. customers, by making it easier to do business and by stimulating the initiative of the private sector:

> Put on a big campaign that says to American businessmen, "You can deal with these folks, as though the border is invisible." Really work on all the red-tape stuff . . . it could open a big market. Because . . . I think there is a tremendous amount of energy, creativity, and ability to create wealth in the private sector in Canada. We have a sort of inferiority complex about business in the private sector here. But [in my company] visitors often go away raving about how good we are. Free trade is not going to help unless something [is done] to break down the psychological and social barriers to getting there.

Generally, it was felt that no government could be expected to make the painful decisions that will help Canada become more competitive (for example, making huge cuts in government expenditures and allowing market forces to reshape the Canadian economy). Although Canada may be in the depths of a structural crisis, the crisis is not widely perceived:

> How are you going to tell people living around Toronto that there is a crisis in Canada? They're not going to believe you.

Thus, the transformation must be achieved piecemeal by business itself: by taking advantage of the falling exchange rate to get a foothold in new markets and expanding from there. In the words of one CEO:

There is not one hell of a lot that we can do here today to make any change in any government's political expediency, high government expenditures, regulations, and other bureaucratic obstacles. But there is sure something that we can do as leaders of our companies. And that is to say, "damn, we are part of a bigger thing. We will do our part!" If, collectively, we instill in ourselves that there is a crisis . . . then something will happen.

Business and Society:
The Double-Edge of the Sword

So what? What *can* be done to remedy Canada's problems in dealing with the challenges of world competition? What *should* be done? Should Canada be prepared to sacrifice things that are distinctively Canadian to achieve a better competitive position? Or should it attempt to preserve its identity and current mode of operation at all costs?

These important questions deeply divided our group of executives, particularly those from business organizations, on the one hand, and those from the educational and human services sectors, on the other.

At the risk of oversimplification the "business view" can be summarized in the following terms:

1. Canada must take up the challenge of becoming competitive in the modern world.
2. Government should do all it can to help, by reducing government expenditures and minimizing or streamlining regulations.
3. Reliance should be placed upon market forces to restructure the economy and social life. Full employment will eventually be achieved, but the restructuring will require many people to develop new skills and to pursue new careers in new locations.

The essence of this position is that if Canadian organizations can become fully competitive in the world economy, other

things will follow: creation of wealth will create new investment, which will create new forms of employment. In the process, Canada will change into a high-tech and service-based economy as automation is used to gain a competitive edge.

The more "socially oriented view" emphasized that the
"competitiveness first" approach would ride roughshod over
precious values. Removal or reduction of social programs and
safety nets would create great social dislocation and distress and
throw the burden of transition on disadvantaged sectors of society: the unemployed, youth, the poor, and less developed re-
gions. The essence of this view was:

1. Canada must balance the need to become more competitive
    with the need to maintain key values.
2. Business must find ways of being more effective within these
    norms.
3. The transition to a new economic structure will create a
    great deal of social dislocation; government social programs
    are essential to provide a buffer in the transition.

These two radically different views reflect a serious polarization in Canada's political culture, for each view has strong
support. Although the business community wants to see competition given free rein, other sectors of society want to keep
business firmly in check. The situation was expressed well by
one (nonbusiness) CEO commenting on the cohesiveness of the
business point of view reflected in group discussion:

> There is a degree of unanimity in the under-
> lying attitudes and values that you are expressing
> . . . which most of the people you talk to most of
> the time share. But you are a hundred and eighty
> degrees from a lot of the values that other people
> from a different slice of society would express. If
> you want to look at a fracture point, and I would
> be very sorry to see this come about . . . [there
> may be] a radical polarization of underlying social
> and political values . . . [that] would be just tragic
> for this country. I think one of the difficulties is

the absence of pluralism, if I can put it that way, in the political and social perspectives in the business community. All your analysis, broadly speaking, converges. But if you took another sector of society, you would have a convergence on quite a different analysis.

The difference in opinion was firm, one side arguing that the socially oriented program was a recipe for "economic suicide" and the other arguing that all that is Canadian is at stake. The dichotomy was expressed well by a CEO from the voluntary sector who summed up the situation in the following terms:

> I feel absolutely schizophrenic, because about half of my life is spent with people like you [business] folks, and the other half of my life is with other groups that are taking [the opposite view]. There is a lot of polarity. So to my mind, there's got to be a way, somehow, to start working at that problem, hooking everything together.

The problem, of course is *how* does one hook everything together? How can one find a way of addressing Canada's weak competitive position, while preserving the core values? The question was addressed in many ways, but with no consensus; for the contradictions seem to run deep.

For example, from a business perspective, one key way to increase one's competitive edge is to replace labor with capital. This trend is evident in the manufacturing sector and has become increasingly visible in the service sector in banks, insurance companies, and other traditionally labor-intensive organizations. Increasing competitiveness has a tendency to create unemployment, thereby reducing domestic purchasing power and, given Canada's "safety nets," adding to government expenditures, which in turn adds to the institutional costs of conducting business and makes it difficult to sustain a competitive edge. As the CEO of a leading manufacturing firm put it:

Unemployment . . . this is a very major issue for the Western world. There is only one way we in Canada can remain competitive and that is to take the labor out of production. If we do that, unemployment is going to remain high. That is true for Canada, and for the States. If this is the case, and governments perceive that they have to [absorb the problem through] support [to] the unemployed, social expenditure, taxation, and thus costs will go up. We have a huge problem.

We are in a vicious circle. But how vicious? The business view hinges on the hypothesis that competitive forces allow the cycle to be broken as the wealth created is used to generate new opportunities, and hence new employment. According to the socially oriented view, it is risky to rely on the assumption that this process is automatic: the money earned through increased competitiveness may not be invested in Canada or in a way that creates jobs for Canadians. Hence the deadlock, which is reflected in the current debate on free trade versus protectionism, and was humorously summarized in one discussion as a choice between "going American" and "going Albanian."

If Canada chooses to "go American," the danger is that it will no longer continue to be Canada. If it chooses to "go Albanian," the protective net it constructs to keep the competition out will lead to atrophy: a falling Canadian dollar, export of capital, decline in productive capacity, falling standard of living, and so on.

The alternative to this polarity is to find creative solutions that, as suggested earlier, "hook" things together so that Canadian organizations improve their competitive position and yet preserve the core social values. This is probably the most important and difficult frontier facing Canadian society at the present time.

Managers have a choice. They can leave it to governments and politicians. Or, they can become active stakeholders in the problem and try to influence the situation, acting as individuals or in concert with other stakeholders.

Contextual Competencies

The remainder of this chapter identifies the key "contextual competencies" that can contribute to this process: building bridges, reframing problems to create new solutions, acting nationally and locally, and developing a new approach to social responsibility. While the focus on Canada continues, the general principles have international application.

Building Bridges

> What we need is the bridge, the change mechanism, the way to innovate, to get to the point where we have a way of pulling together all the [stakeholders] to create a difference.

> The problem with this [bridge building] is that you can't get some groups to buy into . . . any elements of this . . . until there is blood on the floor.

> My view [for Canada] is that there has got to be new partnerships among the various sectors, and I can think of at least four. I think it is time for government, business, labor, and the voluntary sector, at least these four major sectors that all have a high stake in social and economic development, to start working together on some . . . solutions. I think that it is too complicated for any one sector. Government alone—it has been proved time and again—can't solve the problem. And I think that the business sector alone can't solve the problem either. There has to be a joining of forces. It has started, but the attitude of "this is my turf" or "you stay off of my turf" is still so rampant, particularly in the civil service and government, that it is impeding any real effort to find solutions.

Although it was recognized that relations between different groups may be strained and that issues often have to reach a breaking point before cooperation occurs, most executives were in favor of developing active links between different stakeholders wherever possible. Ideas on the bridge-building process varied, from improving communications by "doing a better job at defining issues and shaping opinion" to creating new patterns of interaction and joint initiatives in relation to shared problems.

The importance of this competency is well known. Many organizations are very skilled in this aspect of context management, using various consultative processes to establish and develop dialogue and joint action.

The main insight gained from discussion was that this philosophy of collaboration could be used to generate new attacks on the problem of Canadian competitiveness. For example, there appears to be enormous scope for linking the problems and opportunities facing organizations in different sectors of the economy.

To illustrate this point, take the multitude of problems surrounding the unemployment (or threat of unemployment) created by microprocessing technology. Earlier, we described how this "major issue for the Western world" is creating all kinds of problems in terms of personal and social transformation. Yet, when viewed from an "opportunity" perspective, the changes create many potential areas of growth:

- For education at all levels, for example, to upgrade technical skills and abilities, to create computer literacy, to develop the attitudes that allow people to enjoy challenge and change
- For human services and voluntary organizations, for example, to deal with the problems created by personal and social transformation
- For the software industry, for example, as a key area of development along the lines discussed in Chapter Eight

These growth areas create the opportunity to establish active partnerships among organizations in different sectors of the economy, for example, among business, educational, government, human services, labor, and voluntary organizations.

Of course, problems exist: first, in strengthening links

and finding ways to create and channel resources within and between organizations in different sectors so that all benefit; second, in developing partnerships that respect different value
systems.

Strengthening Links and Rechanneling Resources. How
can links between business, education, human services, and the
voluntary sector be strengthened? As one CEO from the human
services sector observed:

> There are just all kinds of opportunities in
> the human services field . . . to try and get at the is-
> sues raised by unemployment, single-parent fami-
> lies, youth, and other stress points. But there is
> also the problem of burnout of some of our key
> staff people, because we're driving them so hard
> . . . and of limited resources—we simply don't have
> enough. We're trying to put together partnerships
> to work at these issues, involving business, govern-
> ment, and social organizations.

Everyone has a high stake in these problems, which affect
the structure of society itself. For example, youth unemployment represents a lost contribution, and cuts to the heart of
participative democracy because this stratum of society is ex-
cluded and learns not to participate. If resources and ideas can
be channeled to the organizations that deal with this problem,
all sectors benefit. Or, as another example, illiteracy and poor
skills training impact all of society. If people can be provided
the opportunity to improve their education and skills, many different stakeholders will gain. Yet another example: How can
the educational and business sectors make a full and effective
contribution to a country's place in the world economy? Universities, community colleges, and extension study programs can
contribute to a much greater extent in several areas:

- In upgrading skills so that people can rise to the challenge
  created by the introduction of new technologies and new
  styles of organization

- In enhancing the linguistic abilities of those interested in rising to the challenges presented by globalization
- In developing the business and managerial expertise of ethnic groups, so that they can become an integral part of the national effort to penetrate international markets (their natural linguistic abilities constitute a vast, underdeveloped resource!)
- In creating the quality educational institutions (perhaps around the "centers of excellence" concept) that will attract and retain the best faculties and produce intellectual leaders in diverse fields that can help to create a cutting edge
- In producing flexible and imaginative "knowledge workers" who can adapt to different assignments in the emerging "information society"
- In developing the mindsets required for blending the demands of today and tomorrow, making education and re-education a continuing process
- In developing key strategic areas, such as managerial expertise in the software industry, that contribute to a country's role in the world economy
- In helping to develop a proactive, entrepreneurial spirit, especially in small businesses and among young people so that they can find or create niches for new employment (the absence of jobs in large firms makes this an important priority)
- In meeting the educational needs that arise from the changing age structure of the population, particularly the anticipated increase in the proportion of older people

Many executives feel that educational organizations lag in their response to the changes occurring in society:

> They are not reaching out to grasp new opportunities; they are looking to old stakeholders, especially government, as a source of funds.

Many educational organizations are managed from the inside out: they provide the kind of output that *they* want to provide; their internal structures and specialisms largely determine how they relate to the wider environment! As a result, there is often a mismatch between the supply of and demand for educational services. A more outside-in approach, along the lines discussed in Chapter Three, would help to rectify many of the problems. Many of our established educational organizations may be obliged to become more responsive. In the words of one executive, many corporations are "finding that they can do a better job at education than many universities and other similar institutions."

Clearly, educational organizations have much to contribute to the development of a country's position in the world economy, but new approaches may be necessary to unleash this capacity. As discussed with respect to social problems and illiteracy, the potential of organizations in one economic sector to make contributions to organizations in another sector must be unlocked. Conventional arrangements do not work well; new bridges must be built.

Establishing Partnerships That Respect Different Values. It is easy to collaborate on one's own terms; it is much more difficult to do so in situations in which the terms reflect a diversity of values. For example, consider the problems of blending the potential contributions of educational organizations with the needs of the business sector. Educators often resist policies to align education more closely with the needs of business on the premise that education should serve multiple ends and not give too much weight to the needs of a single "client" group. As business attempts to influence education, a significant number of educators withdraw. Those against such policies fear that universities will become "lack[ies] to the business world" or their mission of providing independent, liberal education will be undermined. The overall concern is that one set of values will become dominant over the other.

The same problem is encountered in labor–management relations. Cooperation with management is often viewed as risking incorporation by management, especially when managers define the terms on which cooperation can occur. In building bridges and partnerships among organizations from different sectors, it is necessary to recognize that differing values, opinions, and ideologies will almost certainly arise. And the most robust relationships are those that are built around recognition and respect for those differences. Hence, rather than expecting one side or the other to bend to a particular point of view, it is often much more effective to base arrangements on give and take. The essence of this philosophy was expressed by two CEOs in the following terms:

> We have to strive for understanding, *not* consensus, and a shared view that we belong to the same enterprise and that it is in *everybody's* interest that there be give and take.

> We should be providing a strong voice in terms of bridging [positions], rather than trying to strengthen our side of the argument in the debate to beat the other guy.

Many potential partnerships are blocked because it is difficult to create mutual understanding and define grounds for a mutually satisfactory arrangement.

Reframing Problems to Create New Solutions

Resolution of the issues discussed above necessitates new ways of thinking about conventional problems and interrelations. This ability to reframe existing situations in ways that create new potential for development is a critical competency. It requires recognition that these situations are often associated with mindsets that, if challenged and modified, allow new initiatives to emerge. The process is well illustrated in negotiations in which deadlocks are broken after redefinition of the issues makes new progress possible.

A number of seemingly intractable social and economic issues may be amenable to this reframing. Two such issues are discussed here.

Making Government Expenditures Generative. Government expenditures are often "a drain." Many resources are consumed, and little value or wealth is added; hence, they are a barrier to achievement of a competitive position in the world economy. Is there a way of making government expenditures a truly generative force?

Government monies spent within a country support the economy by increasing levels of consumption. But do they add to investment and productive capacity? Do they create a resource—in terms of a better educated, more highly skilled, and healthier population? Is it possible to make government expenditures more of a resource generator and yet preserve core social values, for example, with respect to adequate safety-net provisions?

These questions cut to the heart of the problem of meeting the needs of a competitive economy in a socially acceptable manner. To the extent that government expenditures contribute to a country's human and technological resource base, the benefits of the tax dollar flow back to the source. The problem is to close the loop between the source and the use of funds. The United States achieves this through heavy defense-related and other expenditures that help build the economic base of the country. The Canadian challenge is to close this loop in a manner consistent with Canadian values, that is, through social, educational, and other expenditures that contribute to technological and human capacities.

Regulating Through Values and Norms. Many aspects of organizational life are regulated by clearly defined rules. Governments control businesses through detailed regulations. Labor-management relations are often codified in page after page of fine print, and organizations often create and apply their own rules for managing relations internally and in relation to the environment. These rules typically create rigidity, foster adversarial relations, and make it difficult for organizations to evolve as rapidly as the environment changes. Is there an alternative way of regulating these relations? Is it possible to work through agreed values and norms rather than detailed rules? Here are some suggestions from the executives involved in my research:

What we need is a shared understanding of the rules of the game, the parameters that you have to deal with, rather than cluttering everything up with bureaucratic regulations!

Governments and bureaucrats need to learn new ways to achieve what they want without passing laws or making threats.

Collaborative attitudes are needed on both sides. Industry has to crank up its ability to speed decision processes and to change. It can expect governments and their bureaucracies to lag. But, this needs to be overcome through collaborative activity. By emphasizing the need for cooperation it may be possible to get at this problem.

A lot of money is put into lobbying for this regulation or that. But no real effort is put into changing the regulatory system itself. We need to give attention to transforming the approach, while protecting the public.

The general idea is that if it is possible to agree on the broad principles that particular sets of regulations strive to achieve, it should be possible to produce a flexible set of arrangements that satisfy the interested parties without hamstringing operations. In Sweden, self-regulation within clearly defined limits often serves as an alternative to close external control. When organizations break agreed limits, severe sanctions are automatically levied. A heavy measure of protection is achieved through a system that is relatively easy to understand and easy to administer.

Value-oriented regulation also has much to offer in the area of labor–management relations. If labor and management could clarify basic ground rules, for example, with respect to security, employment, and other key policies, many detailed regulations would become defunct. As one executive put it:

> I heard a story the other day where a con-
> tractual document [between labor and manage-
> ment] was reduced from over two hundred pages
> to just three. Grievances have almost disappeared.
> Now there's nothing to grieve!

In an adversarial labor–management relations climate,
fine print becomes a weapon used by one side to try to control
the other. It reflects distrust and often *creates* distrust. If one
can get back to basic relationships and principles and build trust
around what is truly important, breakthroughs can be achieved.

Acting Nationally and Locally

To impact issues as complex as those underpinning a
country's weak competitive position, national and local action
is needed. People must develop the networking skills that enable
them to bring together key actors and to orchestrate major interventions at the national and international levels and yet recognize the power and importance of doing what one can locally.

Organizations in virtually all sectors of society are well
versed in the art of national action through labor, trade, and
professional associations, business councils, and industrial coalitions. They are often less skilled in developing coalitions that
span different sectors. In the future, this is likely to become an
important art. Broad-based action is needed to address common
concerns. Coalitions and looser networks that link diverse stakeholders can fulfill this need by mobilizing concern and action
on issues intersectorally, rather than just relying on different
sectors to take separate bites at a problem. The following example of how diverse voluntary organizations are attempting to see
beyond immediate differences to unite and speak in relation to
what they have in common, illustrates this emerging trend and
the scale on which it can occur:

> Over the last ten years major networks of
> about 100,000 voluntary organizations in Canada,
> 56,000 of which are registered charities, have

> emerged. A national coalition has begun to develop
> . . . to network among leaders in a variety of fields
> —health, social work, cultural, international—and
> to engage with governments in various common
> dialogues . . . [about] issues of concern for the
> whole sector. It is the emerging fourth sector in
> our country. There is a great deal of potential and
> a great deal of demand . . . to contribute to the qual-
> ity of social and economic development in Canada.

Canada is in an interesting position to mobilize such action, because its population of individuals and organizations is
small enough to create an impression that one can have an influence. At the same time, there is the problem of "buck passing,"
relying on action at the national level. Hence, the executives involved in discussing this issue placed a strong emphasis on the
idea that each executive must do as much as possible to effect
change locally. Building on the idea that innovation often occurs away from the power centers, they felt that many of the
main initiatives and successes could originate in small, rather
than large, communities and organizations, through people that
are closest to where real action is needed.

A New Approach to Social Responsibility

The competencies described above imply a special relationship with the wider context, a relationship in which the
complex patterns of interdependence that ultimately sustain an
organization are recognized and respected. To build bridges, to
reframe difficult problems, and to blend action at national and
local levels, managers must be sensitive to how the well-being of
the individual organization depends on the well-being of the
whole system. It requires a special sense of social responsibility,
whereby managers recognize that if their organizations are to
succeed, especially in the long term, they must cultivate the
context that will impact their organizations positively.

Social responsibility is usually viewed solely as a matter
of ethics or morality. As such, it is often regarded as an "op-

tional extra," a dimension that may be added to corporate decision making. A more systemic view suggests that social responsibility should be central to how managers think about their relationship with the wider context and approach corporate decision making. Although their effects may seem distant and indirect, the social or "contextual" consequences of corporate decisions ultimately return to influence the organizations that made those decisions. For example, many aspects of poor labor–management relations or of excessive government regulation are responses to corporate actions of the past. The situation can improve only if new ground rules are used to reshape the situation. This requires the ability to identify the values that link and balance the interests of different stakeholders and to implement them as an integral part of business operations.

Many executives involved in discussing this issue believed that social responsibility was no longer a matter of choice. As one CEO put it:

> An indifference to social implications scares
> the public, undermines confidence, and almost al-
> ways ends up backfiring. A real credibility problem
> develops, and this must be avoided at all costs.

However, there was some divergence of opinion with regard to how far this responsibility extends. Some executives emphasized the importance of understanding the issues that are immediately relevant to their organizations. For example, one CEO reported that his firm refused to become involved in businesses that created significant pollution in the environment; another reported that his organization had a conscious policy of not working with the nuclear power industry. In both cases, the concern was minimization of the potentially negative costs and social impacts that might arise from involvement in these highly sensitive areas.

And at the other end of the scale, some executives suggested that organizations should play an active part in shaping national and international issues. For example, it was suggested that if Canadian organizations are truly interested in solving the social problems surrounding structural unemployment or those related to Canada's poor competitive position, then they should face the problem squarely and develop an appropriate plan of action. As one CEO remarked:

> If you want to correct the malaise and determine your future, then figure out what is good. If the problem is that we have a social problem in Canada, too wide a gap between "the haves" and "the have nots," then let's at least figure out how wide our range is here, . . . [and] how much we are going to live within. And that means we are going to pay for it. Then, at least let's do it consciously, put it on the table . . . and get on with it.

The issue of paying the bill was a subject of much discussion. It was recognized that a certain price has to be paid to sustain Canada as a society that cares about its population, and that many corporations play a big role in redistribution of wealth through a high tax dollar. The burning question from a social responsibility standpoint is whether this financial contribution should also be backed by broader and more active recognition of the stake that organizations have in the well-being of society at large.

All the contextual competencies discussed in this chapter require that senior managers become finely tuned to the changes occurring nationally and internationally. In effect, they call for a form of corporate statesmanship that uses outside-in management to create conditions that allow society to flourish. These requirements add pressures and demands to an already demanding role. Even if senior managers confine their attention to the immediate interactions affecting their organization, they can be stretched to the limit. Nevertheless, as discussed earlier, the most important influences on an organization's competitive ability are embedded in the broader context, and it would be foolhardy to ignore them, particularly if they can be influenced and shaped in positive ways.

11

Competence Programs
for Managers
and Their Organizations

In previous chapters, we discussed what senior executives and their organizations must do to ride the waves of change carrying us toward the twenty-first century. It is now time to look at *how* this task can be approached and, in particular, to identify the specific actions through which managers can develop programs that place their organizations at the cutting edge. In this chapter, we focus on three related issues: the competence mindset, strategy-driven competencies, and management education.

The Competence Mindset

At one level, the message of this book is very clear. If organizations wish to be successful in managing the turbulence of the modern world, their managers must develop the skills discussed in previous chapters (see Chapter One for a detailed overview). In particular:

- They will develop skills in *reading the environment, fracture analysis, scenario building,* and other methods to identify the changes relevant to their organizations.
- They will approach the future *proactively,* driving in "forward mode" rather than by looking through the "rear-view mirror." They will anticipate and create change, acting as entrepreneurs rather than bureaucrats. They will manage their

organizations from the *outside in* to sustain an ongoing environmental focus, and use *positioning* and *repositioning* skills to adjust to new opportunities.

- They will recognize the importance of *leadership* and *vision* at all levels of organization, and build direction and commitment around key values and shared understandings.
- They will view their *people as a key resource* and value knowledge, information, creativity, interpersonal skills, and entrepreneurship as much as land, labor, and capital have been valued in the past. They will reorient the economics of their organizations so that human potential is not unduly constrained by short-term financial considerations.
- They will develop *corporate cultures that encourage creativity, learning, and innovation* and develop managerial structures, skills, and processes that promote intelligence and creativity as the life blood of an organization.
- They will replace organizational hierarchies with *flatter, decentralized, self-organizing structures,* in which *facilitation, networking, and remote management* are crucial.
- They will use *information technology as a transformative force,* to create new products and services and to support the decentralized, flatter structures required in flexible, innovative organizations. They will use the technology to promote evolving, "user-driven" information systems and help equip managers with the special interpretive skills required to manage situations of information overload.
- They will develop the skills and attitudes to *manage complexity,* especially the demands of multiple stakeholders, multiple performance objectives, and transition and change.
- They will reshape the environment through development of *contextual competencies* that help to mobilize key actors from different sectors of society in common attacks on shared problems. Networking, creation of alliances, and new methods of tackling old problems will become central concerns of senior management.

The chief executive who asks his or her human resource management staff or organizational development people to review the detailed contents of previous chapters and to assess their relevance to the needs of the organization will find dozens of specific ideas on which action agendas can be based and through which specific aspects of organization and management can be improved. However, there is another level on which these ideas can be approached, for the process of thinking about competence is itself an important competency.

Whenever we address the issue of competency, personal or organizational, we have to think in terms of *what it takes to be effective* in relation to a present or future situation. The very idea of competence encourages an open and dynamic perspective that forces us to address the question of relevance. We may have good skills and abilities, but are they appropriate and effective? We may subscribe to certain values, but how do they resonate with the requirements of the situation? Competence is always a relationship. It depends upon the *appropriateness* of what one is able to do.

The organizations that lead us into the twenty-first century will be those that build a competence mindset into everything they do, focusing on *what it takes to be effective* to reach the cutting edge *and* stay there! They will use this focus to remain open, dynamic, and evolving, invigorating and renewing themselves as they go along. These organizations will have a strong learning orientation, which they will use to develop capacities for self-review and self-renewal, because in a changing environment issues relating to competitiveness, productivity, quality growth, and a host of other key organizational variables hinge on this capacity for intelligent change.

As well as viewing this book as a catalogue of managerial competencies and approaching it with a "shopping list" suited to one's needs, one must also read its "meta-message": it is important that organizations and their managers develop a capacity for self-diagnosis and self-development on an ongoing basis, so that they become competent at being competent!

The C-PLAN: A Process for Developing Strategy-Driven Competence Programs

- Self-diagnosis and self-development!
- Self-review and self-renewal!

- Being open to learning and learning to learn!
- Being competent at being competent!

There are many catchy phrases that describe the overall orientation and thrust of the competence mindset. But how does one bring it into being? How does one develop a capacity for this kind of thinking in oneself and one's organization on an ongoing basis? This is one of the most challenging issues arising from my research. It is fine to glimpse the future and say "that's what we need!" But it is a long road from the observation to the fulfillment of these needs.

Clearly, the competence mindset is in part an attitude that has great affinity to the ideas on proactive management discussed in Chapter Three. A number of executives involved in my competency research forums remarked that for them, the ability to keep their organizations at the forefront of new developments rests on incorporation of this proactive, learning-oriented approach into their key activities. However, there is also much that can be done to develop formal processes that enhance an organization's capacity to assess the competencies it needs on an ongoing basis. These are presented and discussed here as the C-PLAN (the C stands for competence), an approach to competence development that can easily be integrated with the existing planning and development programs within one's organization.

The premise is that a simple "shopping list" approach to managerial competence often results in piecemeal development, with only loose coupling between the competencies developed and the evolving needs of an organization. Good intuitive judgments on the part of those drawing up the list can help to put a fairly sound program together; however, it is much better if the problem can be approached through a more systematic process, building directly from the key strategic issues facing an organization to the detailed competencies required, and from there to the action necessary to bring the competencies into being.

The C-PLAN (see Figure 7) offers a means of achieving this integrated approach to competence development. It uses fracture analysis to create a framework for strategic thinking among senior executives that can then "drive" competence development on

Figure 7. The C-PLAN: A Strategy-Driven Competence Program.

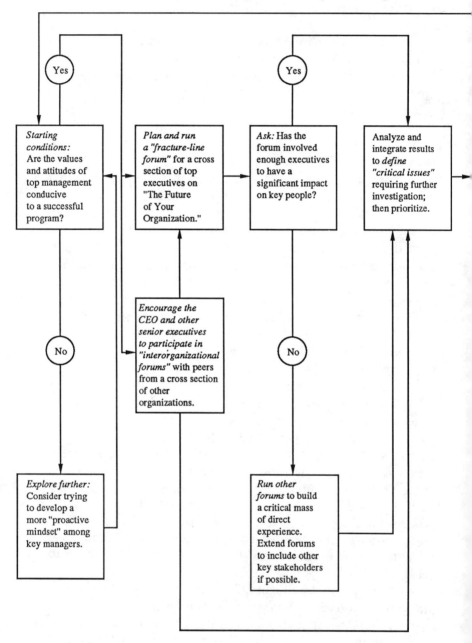

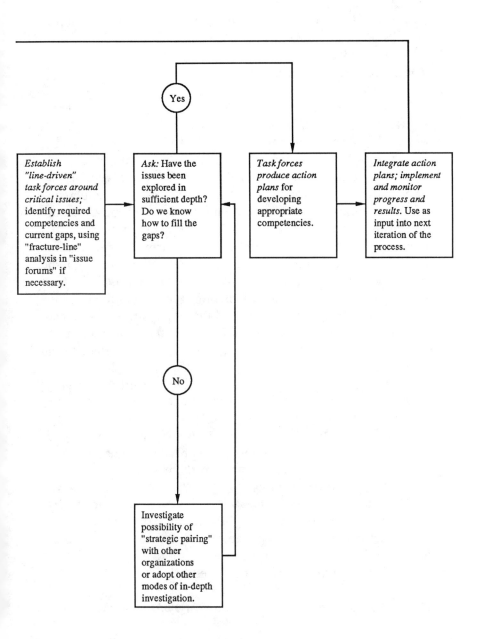

Yes

Establish
"line-driven"
task forces around
critical issues;
identify required
competencies and
current gaps, using
"fracture-line"
analysis in "issue
forums" if
necessary.

Ask: Have the
issues been
explored in
sufficient depth?
Do we know
how to fill the
gaps?

Task forces
produce action
plans for
developing
appropriate
competencies.

Integrate action
plans; implement
and monitor
progress and
results. Use as
input into next
iteration of the
process.

No

Investigate
possibility of
"strategic pairing"
with other
organizations
or adopt other
modes of in-depth
investigation.

an ongoing basis. Figure 7 illustrates the steps in the overall process; its implementation is discussed below.

The Right Starting Conditions

Three conditions are particularly important: support at top levels within the organization; a commitment to a future-oriented approach to management; and opportunities to integrate C-PLAN activities into the organization's strategic thinking.

It is crucial that the CEO and other key executives are "on board," sponsoring C-PLAN activities, as any competency program promoting self-review and self-renewal must be supported by appropriate values and commitments. In particular, it is important that key executives be committed to approaching the future in a future-oriented way rather than "through the rear-view mirror" and be genuinely open to the possibility that an assessment of major environmental trends will raise many issues that challenge current paths of development. As one executive commenting on the C-PLAN put it, "the program tries to get to the guts of what is needed, so it's important that people want to get to the guts."

The person responsible for launching a C-PLAN program must assess the quality of top management support and the prevailing culture and the extent to which key executives are open to the ideas explored in Chapters Two and Three, particularly those relating to fracture analysis and proactive management. It is a good idea to use these chapters as the basis for discussion at an early exploratory meeting, to "test the water" and plant the seeds of the "proactive" approach. It is also a good idea to create formal links between the C-PLAN and the organization's overall approach to strategy development; indeed, it can be launched as part of the organization's approach to the future, using the fracture-line forums discussed below.

Fracture-Line Forums on "the Future of Your Organization"

If the conditions necessary to launch a successful C-PLAN program exist, the process can get off to an excellent start through a series of *fracture-line forums* involving key executives.

These forums should be designed to encourage participants to identify the principal issues likely to shape the future of the organization and to explore the implications of these issues for future competence. Such forums can be supplemented and enriched by ad hoc or ongoing *interorganizational forums* (discussed later) that involve selected executives and are designed to bring additional perspectives, information, and ideas to the overall inquiry process.

These forums require careful design and preparation and expert facilitation. The guidelines are discussed in Appendix A. This communicates the approach required to generate the open-ended and adventurous thinking among participants that moves inquiry in the right direction.

In essence, an attempt is made to create an atmosphere in which short-term concerns are put aside, so that participants can take a longer term view. The goal is to motivate participants to think about their organization from the "outside in," understanding it in the broadest possible context and drawing upon intuition as well as concrete knowledge and observations. A well designed briefing document—outlining the aims of the process and providing information and ideas on key environmental trends or on issues that will stimulate thinking—can play an important part in creating this futuristic perspective. Nevertheless, the key to making these forums a success rests in the use of "fracture-line" methodology to identify potential points of transformation in the wider environment and, hence, the likely impacts on the organization. Dozens of issues may emerge in the process, but with skillful facilitation and synthesis, it is usually possible to develop alternative clusters that highlight key strategic issues. Also, it is often possible to reframe issues and problems so that new insights and approaches emerge.

As an example, the key "fracture line" facing one Canadian organization producing medium high technology products is perceived by key executives as the "new market competition from Japanese organizations." Japanese organizations have made a significant impact on the North American market over the last few years, and a further loss of market share is projected. A competent response is seen to include new initiatives in production, human resource management, marketing, and R&D. However, as discussion proceeds, the problem of Japanese competition is reframed in terms of a more fundamental problem: "innovative capacity" in their *own* organization. They discuss the problems of being innovative and the possibility of developing new products, and they see that the strategies for tackling these problems will require them to reshape relations with the parent company in New Jersey. Given the business parameters that are set in New Jersey, they have little chance of launching an innovation-based recovery; thus, they realize that the strategy to deal with their Japanese competitors lies in creating a new relationship with the parent company. Developing a strategy that New Jersey "will buy" now becomes the focus of attention.

We see here how a discussion of existing and potential "fracture lines" might proceed, and how an understanding and reframing of these fracture lines lead to different interpretations of the strategic issues facing an organization and the priority of different competencies. *Fracture-line forums* encourage executives to reflect on this issue and on the relative priority of putting more time, effort, and money into "beating the competition"; becoming more innovative; or reshaping relations with the head office. This statement oversimplifies the problem facing the organization just discussed, but it does capture the thrust of the C-PLAN approach to competence development.

In a *fracture-line forum* lasting two days, approximately one third of the time would be devoted to identification and discussion of potential fracture lines; the rest would be devoted to the implications of these fracture lines for the future of the organization. The *formal* product of the process would be a document that synthesizes the views of the senior executives as a set of key issues bearing on strategic development (the issues identified through use of the fracture-line methodology) and the beginning of a statement on required managerial competencies. (At this stage it is far more important to identify issues that have a bearing on strategic development than to worry about required competencies, as the latter will be explored later in the process.) The *informal* product of the process is the experience itself. Key executives have thought about their organization in a future-oriented mode and, if the process has been successful, they have gained important insights from the experience. This is crucial, because the process is in many ways as important as the product, helping executives to develop the proactive "outside-in" approach so essential to management in turbulent times. Though the formal agenda of the *fracture-line forum* is to begin development of a competence *plan,* it also helps to develop required competencies among the forum participants.

In a small organization, one forum may be sufficient to launch a successful competency program. In larger organizations, however, several forums involving different groups of executives will be necessary to tap the full range of opinion and expertise and to develop a "critical mass" of people with direct experience of the program. (The more cautious organization can "get its foot in the water" by running one forum and then proceeding with others if it is happy with the results!) Development of this "critical mass" is important in sustaining the thrust of the competency program in the long run and in building a sense of appreciation of the nature and aims of the program within the corporate culture.

At many organizations it is a good idea to extend the process beyond senior management and include a cross section of key stakeholders from within, and perhaps outside, the organization. The greater the variety of knowledge and perspectives built into the process, the richer the result. A broadening of the process also helps to build better understanding and support for the initiatives that emerge. The questions of who to involve and when to involve whom should be considered when the forum is designed.

Defining Critical Issues

Fracture-line forums typically generate a great wealth of information and ideas relevant to an organization's future and a "first-cut" sense of the priority of different issues; however, further work is typically necessary, especially when different forums produce a divergence of opinion. The results of the different sessions need to be integrated; the issues need to be assessed by a representative group of senior executives to identify those of principal importance. These issues are then used to set an agenda for short-term task forces charged with gaining a critical understanding of the issue in question and with developing action plans (see Figure 7).

In a simplified example, suppose that senior executives from the Canadian organization discussed earlier had agreed that the key issues hinge on marketing, creativity and innovation, information technology, and relations between parent and subsidiary. Four short-term task forces would be established, each looking at one issue in depth. These task forces would include some of the executives who participated in the *fracture-line forums* as well as other key stakeholders from within, and perhaps outside, the organization. Each task force would be headed by a senior line manager with a key stake in the issue and would be facilitated and supported by the personnel charged with steering the competency program. It is important that line managers be in the driving seat, because the resulting competency program must resonate with the needs of the "user."

Just as *fracture-line forums* help senior management to uncover strategic issues, more specific *issue forums* can greatly enhance the creative work of task forces using the fracture-line methodology. These *issue forums* help ensure that issues are explored both imaginatively and comprehensively. For example, a task force charged with investigating competencies relating to the marketing function might deal with the issue of what it takes to develop a "market-driven" company (see Chapter Two), as well as issues relating to the marketing function narrowly defined.

Action Plans and an Integrated Competency Program

Under the guidance of facilitators, task forces should produce action plans that document the competencies required to address the key issues emerging from task-force inquiry; the extent to which the organization has, or is currently developing, these competencies; and suggestions for programs that fill the gaps.

In this way, "line-driven" task forces generate the analysis, ideas, and recommendations that provide the foundation of the organization's competency program; however, the integration of this program, its ratification within the organization, and subsequent implementation and monitoring of progress fall on the professional staff responsible for the overall C-PLAN program. Line managers should not be burdened with this task. Their role is to shape the direction and content of the competency program.

As is clear in Figure 7, the preceding discussion captures the overall thrust of the C-PLAN approach, which can be repeated every two to four years, thus creating a process that allows competency development to evolve with time. Two additional aspects of the plan enrich the overall quality of inquiry and results: *interorganizational forums* and *strategic pairing*.

Interorganizational Forums

The process of uncovering key issues can be greatly enriched if the type of inquiry used in *fracture-line forums* is used on an interorganizational basis, through forums that establish ongoing "peer links" between senior executives from a variety of organizations.

In the C-PLAN approach to these forums, clusters of organizations that may have something to contribute to each other are identified; then parallel groups of CEOs, top organizational strategists, or especially gifted executives arrange to meet on a regular basis to address the issues relevant to their organizations. The purpose is to encourage dialogue among talented people who have different skills and perspectives and who feel free to discuss important issues with equals in an environment of trust and confidentiality. These forums are "executive driven" in that the participants provide the main source of information and learning. Though facilitated by staff with expertise in running such forums (see Appendix A), the aim of these forums is to create an environment of shared investigation and mutual problem solving. At one meeting the focus may be "the future" and the "fracture lines" influencing the organizations represented. At another meeting, the focus may be a specific problem facing one of the executives in the group. Whatever the focus, the same principle applies: properly facilitated, these sessions provide environments in which participants learn to solve the problems facing their organizations as they address the problems faced by other organizations. These forums, therefore, are not "elite clubs" or "therapy sessions" for hard-pressed executives; they are executive learning systems, and they serve a number of important functions. Specifically, they

- Provide an opportunity for senior executives to reflect and to place issues relating to "the future" firmly on their agenda.
- Provide excellent opportunities for managers to develop an "outside-in" perspective on their organization. By viewing an organization as others see it, or by listening to developments outside the usual frame of reference, novel insights often emerge. The process can help a manager challenge fundamental assumptions of current practice.
- Provide an ideal setting in which to learn more about the contextual competencies discussed in Chapter Ten and to develop the alliances that may help to forge new attacks on shared problems. Executive forums at the CEO level have a particularly important role here, because they can help participants understand their organizations more holistically and help them to rethink strategy.

As generators of executive learning, *interorganizational forums* have a powerful role in developing the competence of senior executives and in generating important knowledge and insights that directly contribute to other elements of the C-PLAN program presented in Figure 7.

Strategic Pairing

Another means of injecting special expertise and insight into the C-PLAN program is found in what I call *strategic pairing*. On certain issues the "line-driven" task forces established to investigate competency development may find that they do not have the experience or perspective necessary to investigate the issues at hand. In such situations, it may be possible to forge links with another organization, in a manner that is mutually beneficial. For example, in developing its information-management systems, a consumer products firm seems to have exhausted its ability to create exactly what it needs using its existing technology. The C-PLAN task force charged with investigating the future of information technology in the organization quickly comprehends the situation and, rather than accept present constraints, looks for a new input to task-force deliberations. It is at this stage that some form of strategic pairing with another organization can generate major benefits. It may be possible to establish a special relationship with the computer hardware supplier or with a software company, who can initiate a project focusing on the firm's problems. Although the consumer products firm stands to gain from the computer firm's expertise, the computer firm can also, perhaps, learn much from its customer's problems, by formulating solutions that serve as prototypes for solving problems elsewhere or by gaining insights that help it to refine its own products and services. The consumer products firm's problem provides an opportunity for the computer firm to learn more about its market and the effectiveness of its product design.

In another example, a large public utility assigns a C-PLAN task force to investigate the problem of managing relations with key external stakeholders; the participants realize that great progress can be made by establishing a series of paired relations, or a consortium of key stakeholders, to explore issues firsthand. As in the case of the consumer products firm discussed above, the new linkage allows the participants to get inside each other's thinking and address particular problems in a mutually beneficial manner. As well as bringing to light the competencies necessary to manage stakeholder relations in the future, strategic pairing actually helps to bring these competencies into being.

If developed as a major thrust of a C-PLAN program, strategic pairing can be systematically used to explore the consequences of particularly difficult fracture lines from a novel perspective.

Benefits of the C-PLAN

The C-PLAN is an extremely comprehensive means of developing managerial competencies. It can be an integral part of an organization's ongoing learning and development and can enhance the quality and productivity of a wide range of organizational activities on a continuous basis. The process offers a number of specific benefits:

- It provides a strategy-driven approach to the development of future competencies, ensuring that programs and priorities are kept "in sync" with an organization's evolving needs. The senior managers, who are ultimately responsible for guiding the organization, uncover the issues that provide a framework within which future competence is developed. These issues "drive" the competency program on an ongoing basis. Under the C-PLAN, therefore, the possibility of senior management taking one road and human resource management and organizational development another is minimized. The "fad approach" to competence development, in which programs swing from one focus to another for no coherent reason, is also minimized. A change in direction of competence development under the C-PLAN implies a change in strategic direction, and must be supported by a rationale at the most basic level.
- The process also helps to build shared understanding, ownership, and commitment among key members of the organization. This is critical in creating the momentum needed to ensure that strategic priorities impact daily practice. Many organizations flounder because the strategic thinking of senior managers does not impact the core culture of the organization. The C-PLAN counters this possibility through various mechanisms that link strategic thinking with competence development programs that foster appropriate mindsets, values, and attitudes on a daily basis.
- By including a wide range of people in the forums and task forces, the C-PLAN minimizes opposition to key initiatives. So often, organizational politics stall or sabotage important developments. The C-PLAN provides an opportunity to debate and to develop initiatives that circumvent potential problems so that the proposed programs are improved.
- Because the task forces responsible for translating strategic

initiatives into concrete action plans are driven by line executives with a high stake in producing practical outcomes, the C-PLAN is finely tuned to produce results that are "in sync" with the organization's evolving needs. Human resource management and organizational development staff may play a key role in orchestrating and implementing the process, but their role is one of support rather than direction. Line managers drive the action plans, ensuring that prioritization is effective and that important gaps are filled.

- The C-PLAN overcomes a major problem for human resource management and organizational development staff. Often these executives are perceived to be in a "selling role" —trying to convince line managers about the existence of particular needs or the worth of particular programs or development packages. Under the C-PLAN these professionals have a means of developing human and organizational resources in a strategic, yet nondirective, way. The C-PLAN provides a strategy for human resource management and organizational change, because it is the source of a widely based set of initiatives that can identify and address all the key issues that normally fall within the mandate of professionals working in these areas.

- Finally, and of crucial importance, the C-PLAN *process* is also one of its most important *products.* Many of the activities in which executives participate, notably those generated by the forums and task forces, actually lead to development of important competencies. In addition to fulfilling specific needs, they serve as management development programs. The whole C-PLAN process itself represents a proactive "outside-in" approach to management, encouraging managers to identify key fractures before they occur and acquire the skills necessary to deal with them. Rather than looking back at what other organizations are doing, an organization is encouraged to focus on its own situation and to decide what it must do to meet the challenge of its own unique set of circumstances. In offering the means through which this goal can be accomplished, the process creates an atmosphere that promotes continuous self-review and self-renewal.

Implications for Management Education

Finally, in terms of a general conclusion, we come to the broad implications of my research for management education, whether provided by in-house training schemes, business schools, or private sector programs. Clearly, there are many ways that the ideas discussed can be used to reshape the agenda of many current programs—both in terms of content and general thrust.

Traditionally, most educational programs have emphasized the importance of functional processes and skills: planning, marketing, accounting, finance, MIS, human resource management, communications, time management, and so on. The thrust of my work suggests that these processes and skills are important, but to be fully effective their use needs to be framed by a broad appreciation of the context in which they are to be used and of their potential impacts. For example, in learning about planning, managers need to be keenly aware of the difference between proactive and reactive approaches and of the relevance of the former in dealing with a turbulent world. In learning about accounting systems and management control, managers must be aware of the implications for innovation and human resource development. In designing information-management systems, they need to be aware of the transformative potential of the new technology, and how such systems can stifle or promote development. In improving the efficiency of their organization, they need to appreciate the likely impact on the wider context and to learn how to avoid potential negative consequences.

The skills needed to enrich management education are the "mindset skills" that sustain this capacity to assess the relevance and implications of what one is doing—so that one becomes competent at being competent. In my view, this is the competency that managers will ultimately need to ride the waves of change leading into the twenty-first century, and which future management education programs must help to provide.

Appendix A:
Designing C-PLAN Forums

The purpose of this Appendix is to outline the principles that can be used to design and implement C-PLAN executive forums, such as the *fracture-line forums,* which allow executives to think about the future from a broad perspective, the *interorganizational forums,* which involve CEOs and other senior executives from a range of organizations, and the *issue forums,* which are conducted as part of task force activities. In line with C-PLAN objectives, these forums seek to expand horizons while maintaining an action focus. The following eight guidelines seem particularly important.

Defining an Appropriate Mindset

When busy executives are asked to spend any length of time on an issue, they usually like to have a clearly defined mandate or at least some evidence that their efforts will be productive. This mindset encourages an *action* focus, which usually works against a more open-ended exploration of issues. Therefore, top-level forums must be designed to nurture an open, future-oriented mindset among participants. The C-PLAN can help communicate the broad aim of the process, but cultivation of the right mindset is a situation-specific problem, as the attitudes of executives vary enormously. Some may relish "the unusual"; others may respond more positively to fairly "traditional" briefings.

A well-designed briefing document can help executives get outside their usual frames of reference to explore some of the broader changes that may influence their organization. My approach is to create a document that communicates the aims of the C-PLAN process and marshals the evocative information and ideas that will stimulate thinking about the future. This document might include a delineation of key environmental trends—such as in Figure 2 (Chapter Two)—or articles that are relevant to the future of the organization. Preforum preparation could include reading all, or selected chapters, of this book. The only firm rule is to design for the specific situation being confronted. The manner in which an executive forum is introduced to participants before they arrive is critical and warrants a great deal of careful attention.

Recognizing the Importance of Variety

A law of cybernetics, known as "the law of requisite variety," states that a system can cope with the demands of its environment only if its internal adaptive mechanisms are at least as diverse as that environment. An important implication for the design of learning systems is that adequate variety should always be built into their infrastructure. This means that with respect to group learning processes, it is far wiser to draw participants from a variety of domains rather than assemble people who have much in common. Groups comprising like-minded individuals quickly develop convergence and symptoms of "group-think." They become trapped by their favored frames of reference. In contrast, groups composed of dissimilar individuals can be energized by internal differences and, if appropriately focused and facilitated, can generate powerful, open-ended, and evolving patterns of learning.

This principle must be kept firmly in mind in designing all forums and task forces associated with C-PLAN activities. For example, *fracture-line forums* must be organized to represent the broadest range of opinion possible. These forums should include the CEO and senior executives drawn from diverse parts

of the organization, so that different perspectives can be brought
to bear on discussion of any given environmental trend or corporate problem. Whenever possible, they should be extended to
include all organizational stakeholders who can make a valuable
contribution. Similarly, *interorganizational forums* work best
when they include peers from a range of very different organizations. The greater the representation of different segments of
business and society, the better, because the ideas and expertise
from one sector can enrich another. C-PLAN *task forces* must
also include a cross section of people with a stake in the issue at
hand, including people from operational and managerial levels
and trade union representatives.

The potential for learning increases as the diversity of
backgrounds, knowledge, values, and biases increases; however,
the increased diversity often necessitates strong skills in conflict
management. The process designer must be aware of these problems and trade-offs and of the range of difference that can be
built into a group. For example, the issue of confidentiality, or
the "comfort level" of executives, must always be kept in mind.

Other trade-offs have to be made in relation to the size of
the group versus the variety represented. Small groups of six or
seven are ideal for in-depth discussion, but this may mean exclu-
sion of an important element of the variety needed to tackle an
issue. Larger groups, on the other hand, change the interpersonal
dynamics, creating room for participants "to hide" for long
periods of time and become less involved. Again, the process designer must make important judgments to create an effective
arrangement.

An Empowering, Action-Oriented Focus

Whenever one attempts to address complex issues there is
always a danger that one will become completely overwhelmed
and, psychologically, end up in a worse position than when one
started. This is particularly true in addressing issues concerning
the future, for this topic is so intangible and, potentially, of
unbounded complexity. For example, consider the map of envi-

ronmental forces presented in Figure 2 (Chapter Two). The forty-seven trends represented there do not provide the complete picture of the modern environment, but they do serve to illustrate the enormity of the problem facing senior executives concerned with assessing the significance of environmental change for their organization. There are more than two thousand potential lines of *direct* interaction among the forty-seven trends. The different trends cluster and impact each other in a variety of ways. Thus, attempts to analyze these trends often have a paralyzing effect, as the analyzer typically is ensnared in the complexity. Rather than clarifying the situation, it merely emphasizes the impossibility of the task.

From an early stage, therefore, the process designer must try to help senior executives cut through the complexity in an action-oriented manner. He or she must find ways of empowering rather than overpowering. It is here that the fracture-line methodology becomes so important; it provides a means of opening up issues in a manageable way. Optimism, achievement, and a sense that the process is worthwhile must be generated. And ways have to be found of creating a situation in which the participants (rather than the facilitator) provide the main momentum behind the inquiry process. The design process is challenging, as genuine learning and development always require a degree of openness, which often runs counter to the desire of participants, and often facilitators, to achieve closure. The secret rests in motivating the members of the forum or task force so that *they* take ownership and make the most of the running. When *they* are "in charge," spectacular results often emerge!

Creating the Right Amount of Structure

Evident in the preceding section is the problem of striking a balance between "structure" and "openness" in project design. There are powerful psychological forces at work in project design that often lead designers to incorporate too much structure. This can constrain inquiry and short-circuit important group dynamics. The discussion of complex problems is rarely linear. Ideas tend to bounce around in many directions, diving below the surface and reemerging later in a new form. Facilitators must have a clear vision of their goals and must act on clear principles to help produce a successful outcome, but they must also avoid creating too rigid a framework.

An agenda is needed, but it must be loose and flexible. A means of assessing progress is also necessary, but it must be tolerant of the often winding nature of progress. And above all else, close attention must be given to sustaining credibility: if the designers/facilitators appear credible, the participants will tolerate ambiguity to a greater extent.

To achieve this last aim, considerable attention must be given to the briefing document introducing the process and to the introductory presentation that initiates the forum or task force. If credibility can be firmly established at this stage, there is less pressure on the facilitators to make an impression as the process proceeds. This is an important consideration in facilitating groups of powerful individuals, as the facilitator is often the lowest on the totem pole.

Skills of Active Facilitation

In addressing complex problems in group settings, participants often hit major roadblocks that can easily overwhelm and reduce the energy of the group. Facilitators must be alert to this possibility and adopt a style that allows them to intervene in an active rather than a passive manner.

The task of facilitating C-PLAN forums usually comprises four functions, each requiring special skills.

1. The need to *manage group process.*
    - Understanding the social and psychological dynamics within the group
    - Sustaining a task-related focus
    - Managing time
    - Knowing when to encourage speculation and creativity or a more disciplined integration of ideas
    - Knowing when and how to end a particular session so that participants have a sense of optimism and energy for the next step in the process
2. The need to adopt *a reflective, synthesizing approach to*

group discussion that summarizes and "mirrors" issues back to the group, so that they are able to remember and integrate their ideas or deal with the paradoxes that have been raised.

3.   The need to make *interventions that "frame" and "reframe" the issues,* especially as a means of unblocking overheated or unproductive discussions or of energizing excessively myopic or "groupthink" discussions.

4.   The need to make an *unobtrusive record* of group discussion, so that all relevant insights can be retrieved and fed back into later discussion, or made part of a formal report. Some facilitators are blessed with a great memory; others are skilled in flip-charting or note-taking; others are able to combine elements of these approaches, perhaps with a backup tape recording.

These four functions usually demand the involvement of two facilitators adopting an interactive style: one facilitator is responsible for functions 1, 2, and 4; the other focuses on function 3. This approach allows for powerful interventions where the first facilitator moderates the proceedings, and the second facilitator becomes an active member of the group. In this role, he or she can become fully involved with the *content* of the discussion: intervening to energize discussions, for example, by drawing out the variety of ideas and attitudes within the group; arguing points and counterpoints to promote constructive exploration of issues; and generally encouraging that type of thinking that allows the group to break through problems and barriers.

This dual facilitation is a team-based approach. Although both facilitators are concerned with the quality of the process as a whole and may at times intervene in relation to each other's functions, the division of focus creates a powerful synergy.

Synthesis, Framing, and Reframing

In the design of a relatively unstructured group discussion, it is vitally important to build opportunities for the synthesis, framing, and reframing of issues. Group discussion can jump from one issue to another, sometimes at great loss of continuity and in-depth development of key themes. Thus, it is important to ensure that lost ideas resurface and to develop a means of presenting them so that they tap into key issues. As well, discussion must be energized so that artificial constraints and blindspots are challenged and put in new perspective, especially in ways that communicate a sense of the possible.

The ability to create time for synthesis and reorientation of discussion is also important. The good facilitator should always keep track of key issues and make "on-line" interventions that frame and reframe debate to achieve productive results; however, there is usually no substitute for the breakthroughs that can be achieved when a significant block of time is set aside between group sessions to synthesize and reframe the raw material generated in discussion. Sometimes it is possible to design processes in which the participants themselves perform this function. Even so, strong arguments can be made in favor of strong facilitator intervention or assistance in the synthesizing and reframing process.

A Design That Evolves Within Critical Parameters

The design and implementation of high-level executive forums are as much a question of mindset as of protocol. The methodology hinges on developing and implementing a process oriented by key parameters, rather than a set of rules. These parameters, which have been discussed above, require a clear vision of what one is trying to achieve as well as an openness that allows each discussion group to evolve in its own way.

This openness requires a degree of considered risk taking, guided by a sensitivity for emerging group processes. Designers/ facilitators must thus be open to continuous experimentation and be wary of achieving "the perfect design" that will work in the same way in all situations. It is usually more effective to prepare oneself for the process by becoming aware of potential pitfalls and how to avoid them—by thinking through and engaging in trial "dry runs"—than to try to predesign a perfect outcome. Somewhat paradoxically, it is necessary to have a clear conception of the design of a project, but it must be recognized that the design is no more than a starting point that will need to be modified to meet the unfolding contingencies of a given situation. Continuous design and redesign, rather that rigid pre-design, is the rule.

Documentation of Results

Finally, great care must be devoted to recording the substance of forums and task forces, to capture the essence of discussion *and* create an action momentum. In the C-PLAN, the output of one stage becomes the input for another, so it is vitally important that designers/facilitators be effective summarizers and integrators. Often, the output of a particular meeting may need clarification or refinement if an appropriate quality and momentum are to be sustained.

Considerable attention also needs to be devoted to systematization of the learning process for future project designs. Codification of ideas or tactics that worked or failed and ongoing review and evaluation of process design can do much to develop and disseminate the principles that will help provide the basis for future success.

Appendix B:
Notes on the
Research Methodology

When first asked whether I would be interested in studying "emerging managerial competencies" as part of a Shell Canada research study at York University, I remember thinking "I'll need a crystal ball!" The emphasis of the project was on *emerging* competencies: the competencies that would be needed by managers in the 1990s and beyond. This seemed to present a special problem. How can one know what the future holds? The past can be reviewed and the present observed, but how does this knowledge lead to an understanding of future needs? I thought it might be possible to identify competencies that are in the planning stage and do some forecasting, or conduct a survey and ask managers what they thought might happen. However, these tactics would produce little that managers did not already know, falling short of the requirements of the research project.

It is against this background that I looked at the possibility of using an action-learning methodology to study the problem. This approach to research has a long but somewhat unheralded history (see, for example, Argyris, Putnam, and Smith, 1985; Emery, 1982; Lewin, 1951; Morgan and Ramirez, 1984; Ramirez, 1983; Revans, 1971, 1982; Trist, 1976, 1982). Also, I had already investigated the possibility of using action-learning techniques to create "learning systems" capable of addressing what Russell Ackoff (1974) has called "messes": complex networks of problems characterized by so many sets of interrelations that it is difficult to grasp the problems as wholes. It struck me that the idea of trying to say something useful about emerging managerial competencies fell into this class of problems. (The reason is obvious when one reflects on the interconnections among the trends illustrated in Figure 2 in Chapter Two.)

The Action-Learning Approach to Research

Action learning typically has a dual objective: (1) of producing an original research output (2) through a process that is of direct practical value to those involved. This approach differs from more conventional research methods where knowledge is pursued as an end in itself. The emphasis is on *action* and *learning,* on creating knowledge that helps to address specific issues and problems in an actionable way. The special character of this approach is that it generates knowledge through the design of a learning process that itself proves to be a means for approaching and "solving" the problems being addressed. In other words, the medium of the research is part of its message.

Over the years the aspects of the action-learning approach have been applied to a wide range of situations:

- To generate individual and group learning, as in Revans's (1982) approach to management education and problem solving
- To generate organizational change and development, as in Argyris and Schön's (1978) approach to the development of learning systems and in the Tavistock approach to action research (Trist, 1976, 1982)
- To create broader systemic changes in relation to Ackoff-type "messes," as in the use of search-conferencing methodology to address such community and social problems as hunger in the Third World (Morley and Ramirez, 1983), community revitalization in depressed local economies (Trist, 1982), and other broad social experiments (Emery and Emery, 1976; Emery, 1982; Morgan and Ramirez, 1984; Williams, 1982)

Requirements of the Managerial Competency Project

The managerial competency research project offered an opportunity to interweave and develop aspects of this previous work. Although the mandate was to develop a study that would have relevance on a systemwide basis—by contributing to our understanding of managerial competence and the demands of the future in the most general sense—there was also the expectation that the results should contribute to the effectiveness of individual managers and the organizations for which they worked.

Because the project focused on general managerial competencies, rather than industry- or organization-specific competencies, it was initially thought that the "search conference" method would prove to be the most appropriate. Search conferences typically proceed by assembling for two to five days a diverse group of forty-five to fifty people who have a stake in the issues to be explored, motivating these people to think about the contrast between desired and likely futures, and encouraging them to think about the actions that must be taken to make their desired future a reality.

The aim of such a process is to create a novel learning system by encouraging participants to look at situations in new ways and thereby create new action initiatives. When the process is carefully designed and facilitated, it often results in important breakthroughs on difficult problems (see Emery, 1982; Morley, 1987, for detailed discussions).

As the search conference method was explored, it seemed to offer many opportunities. It was a means of involving senior executives in discussions about the future, and perhaps most importantly, it focused attention on the gaps between present competencies and future requirements, thus creating an action perspective that could help effect these future competencies. However, there also seemed to be problems. Search conferences usually work best when the issue under investigation is of pressing importance to those involved. It takes a deep commitment to sustain the long, and at times frustrating, process of inquiry.

Did the issue of future managerial competencies command this degree of concern among senior executives? Was it possible to produce results that would satisfy the diverse needs of all participants? It was a hairline decision. Yes, one could "pull it off." However, there was a real danger that the process would fall short of its potential. The challenge was to find a means of preserving the advantages of search conference methodology by designing a process that would overcome these problems.

Project Methodology

It was against this background that the project team (Gareth Morgan and Wayne Tebb) with the help of an advisory committee (Alan Hockin, Bill Menzel, and Rein Peterson from York University, and Bob Taylor and Doug Wade from Shell Canada) took up the challenge. In line with the action-learning approach, we realized that the research method would itself be one of the important products of the research process, so enormous effort was devoted to the exploration and design of alternatives.

This effort began with Morgan and Tebb trying to put themselves in the positions of CEOs charged with examining the general implications of the future for their organizations. The task quickly became overwhelming; there seemed to be no end to the trends that had to be taken into consideration. In the process of exploring and documenting some of those trends (summarized in Figure 2, Chapter Two), it quickly became evident that some means of cutting through the complexity was needed. Analysis led to paralysis! We had to find a method of dealing with complexity that empowered us.

The search for an empowering methodology led to the idea of looking for "fracture lines" that had the power to transform one's organization. Besides capturing what many effective strategists do intuitively, fracture-line methodology provided a means of approaching discussion of "the future" in a precise and action-oriented way. The concept is obviously relevant to improving the strategic thinking in any organization and, thus, was made the linchpin of the project. We also realized that thinking about "fracture lines" could prove important in defining the open-ended yet action-oriented mindset that would be required from the executives participating in the research.

Once the fracture-line approach had been selected as a means of structuring the project, we were faced with designing a group process in which it could be used. The wisdom distilled from this experience is now codified in the eight principles for designing executive forums presented in Appendix A.

These principles were derived from the research team's prior knowledge of action-learning methodology (see, for example, Morgan and Ramirez, 1984) and from the experience gained in applying these principles to the problems at hand. As in most action-learning projects, the methodologies had to be developed and refined to serve the evolving needs of the situation.

The Method in Practice

The key decision in the evolution of the methodology was to use a group "inquiry process" involving six to ten senior managers rather than a large search conference format. These senior executives from a variety of organizations were invited to spend a day and a half discussing the trends and forces influencing their organizations using the fracture-line methodology, and identifying emerging managerial competencies. The executives were divided into three groups as outlined in Table 1.

Prior to the discussion, all executives received briefing documents that introduced the fracture-line methodology and described the general aims of the project. They were provided with a review of the forty-seven trends illustrated in Figure 2 (Chapter Two) and were asked to consider how these trends were influencing, or were likely to influence, their organizations. Each discussion group was then organized and facilitated in accordance with a common plan incorporating the eight principles discussed in Appendix A.

The executives were encouraged to bring *their* views and concerns to the discussion table and explore them as openly as possible. To achieve this, each discussion group was scheduled for six sessions:

Table 1. Comparison of the Three Discussion Groups.

Sectors Represented	
Group 1: Presidents of small companies and leading vice-presidents from large and medium-sized firms	Automobile manufacturing Computer software Food products Import and distribution Insurance Pharmaceuticals Oil industry
Group 2: Chief executives of large organizations	Automotive parts manufacturing Banking Chemicals Computer manufacturing and systems design Consumer products University Voluntary sector and human services
Group 3: Leading vice-presidents from large organizations	Electronic products manufacturing Insurance Minerals and natural resources Oil industry Real estate and development University business school
Total number of executives = 20	

Session I: Discussion began around a predetermined agenda. The project facilitators provided a brief "orienting statement" on the nature of the project and the fracture-line concept, and group members were asked to comment on how the three following developments in the business world were impacting their organization and their industry.

1. The introduction of microprocessing
   a. Computer-assisted manufacturing (CAM) and computer-assisted design (CAD)
   b. Automated offices
   c. Just-in-time systems of management
2. Changing product profiles
   a. Development of "smart" (information-rich) products and production processes
   b. Development of "peripherally driven systems" ("user

driven" rather than "centrally driven," for example,
localized heating and air control in large offices,
automated banking services)
   c. Shorter product life cycles and payback periods
3. Changing bases of competitive advantage
   a. Low-cost production
   b. Ability to deal with the market as a driving force
   c. Knowledge and creativity as key resources
   d. "Response capacities" and ability to deal with change
and discontinuity

Session II. This session was designed to let the executives
begin to shape the agenda of discussion. All were asked to identify five or six fracture lines that seemed to be impacting their
organizations. The concerns raised in this and the previous session were synthesized overnight by the research team into groups
of focal issues that captured the essence of the discussions. An
abbreviated list of these issues is presented in Table 2.

Sessions III, IV, and V. These focal issues then provided a
launch pad for more detailed discussion and analysis of future
managerial competencies. Each of the three issues generated
much debate about both general and specific implications.

Session VI. This final session focused on generating additional thoughts and comments on future competencies.

In this way, discussion was organized to maximize executive input; the facilitators intervened to remove potential roadblocks, to attend to process problems, to synthesize when necessary, and, generally, to energize and empower the group effort
(the detailed principles used are described in Appendix A).

Project Results

The proceedings of these group discussions form the substance of this book. The details on emerging managerial compe-

Table 2. Focal Issues Emerging from Group Discussions.

Group 1	Group 2	Group 3
The impact of information technology	Developing organizational capacities to learn, to change, to innovate, to synthesize	Sustaining a market orientation (in the sense of staying in touch with a changing environment)
Weak Canadian competitive position	Weak Canadian competitive position	The challenge of globalization
The relationship between unemployment and lost markets	The possibility of a growing polarization in Canadian society	The management of complexity

tencies are presented in Chapters One to Ten. The insights that emerged from development of the project methodology form the core of the C-PLAN discussed in Chapter Eleven. In this way, the research has attempted to achieve the two objectives of an action-learning project.

References

Ackoff, R. L. *Redesigning the Future.* New York: Wiley, 1974.

Alperovitz, G., and Faux, J. *Rebuilding America.* New York: Pantheon Books, 1984.

Alston, J. P. "Japan as Number One? Social Problems of the Next Decades." *Futures,* 1983, *15,* 342–356.

Argyris, C., Putnam, R., and Smith, D. M. *Action Science: Concepts, Methods, and Skills for Research and Intervention.* San Francisco: Jossey–Bass, 1985.

Argyris, C., and Schön, D. *Organizational Learning: A Theory of Action Perspective.* Reading, Mass.: Addison-Wesley, 1978.

Badaracco, J. L., and Yoffie, D. B. " 'Industrial Policy': It Can't Happen Here." *Harvard Business Review,* 1983, *61,* 96–105.

Bassuk, E. "The Homelessness Problem." *Scientific American,* 1984, *251,* 40–45.

Beckman, R. C. *The Downwave: Surviving the Second Great Depression.* New York: Dutton, 1983.

Benjamin, R., and Kudrie, R. T. (eds.). *The Industrial Future of the Pacific Basin.* Boulder, Colo.: Westview, 1984.

Berkowitz, W. R. *Community Impact: Creating Grassroots Change in Hard Times.* Cambridge, Mass.: Schenkman, 1982.

Bezold, C. (ed.). *Pharmaceuticals in the Year 2000: The Changing Context for Drug RD.* Alexandria, Va.: Institute for Alternative Futures, 1983.

Blackburn, M. L., and Bloom, D. E. "What's Happening to the Middle Class?" *American Demographics,* 1985, *7,* 18–25.

Bodley, J. H. *Victims of Progress.* Palo Alto, Calif.: Mayfield, 1982.

Brooks, H., Liebman, L., and Schelling, C. (eds.). *Public–Private Partnership: New Opportunities for Meeting Social Needs.* Cambridge, Mass.: Ballinger, 1984.

Brown, L. R. *State of the World 1984: A Worldwatch Institute Report on Progress Toward a Sustainable Society.* New York: Norton, 1984.

Brown, L. R., and Wolf, E. C. *Soil Erosion: Quiet Crisis in the World Economy.* Washington, D.C.: Worldwatch Institute, 1984.

Bugliarello, G. "Hyperintelligence: The Next Evolutionary Step." *The Futurist,* 1984, *18,* 6–11.

Carnoy, M., Shearer, D., and Rumberger, R. *A New Social Contract: The Economy and Government After Reagan.* New York: Harper & Row, 1983.

Delamaide, D. *Debt Shock: The Full Story of the World Credit Crisis.* New York: Doubleday, 1984.

Diamond, E., Sandler, N., and Mueller, M. *Telecommunications in Crisis: The First Amendment, Technology, and Deregulation.* Washington, D.C.: Cato Institute, 1983.

Drobnick, R. "America's Growing International Debt." *The Futurist,* 1984, *18,* 18–20.

Dror, Y. "Governance Redesign for Societal Architecture." *World Future Society Bulletin,* 1984, 17–24.

Drucker, P. F. *Managing in Turbulent Times.* New York: Harper & Row, 1980.

Drucker, P. F. "The New Meaning of Corporate Social Responsibility." *California Management Review,* 1984, *26,* 53–63.

Emery, F. E., and Emery, M. *A Choice of Futures.* Leiden, Netherlands: Nijhoff, 1976.

Emery, M. *Searching for New Directions, in New Ways, for New Times.* Canberra: Australian National University, 1982.

Frank, A. G. "Can the Debt Bomb Be Defused?" *World Policy Journal,* 1984, *5,* 723–743.

Gilmore, T., Krantz, J., and Ramirez, R. "Action Based Modes of Inquiry and the Host–Researcher Relationship." *Consultation,* 1986, *5,* 160–176.

Ginsberg, N., and Lalor, B. A. *China: The '80s Era.* Boulder, Colo.: Westview, 1984.

Goldhar, J. D., and Jelinek, M. "Plan for Economies of Scope." *Harvard Business Review,* 1983, *61,* 141–148.

Gordon, T. J. "Global Consequences of Improving Productivity." *Technological Forecasting and Social Change,* 1983, *24,* 107–124.

Hamrin, R. D. *A Renewable Resource Economy.* New York: Praeger, 1983.

Hawken, P. *The Next Economy.* New York: Ballantine, 1983.

Hawken, P., Ogilvy, J., and Schwartz, P. *Seven Tomorrows: Toward a Voluntary History.* New York: Bantam, 1982.

Hayden, D. *Redesigning the American Dream: The Future of Housing, Work and Family Life.* New York: Norton, 1984.

Hayes, R. H., and Wheelwright, S. C. *Restoring Our Competitive Edge: Competing Through Manufacturing.* New York: Wiley, 1984.

Henriksson, B. *Not for Sale: Young People in Society.* Aberdeen, England: Aberdeen University Press, 1983.

Hills, L. D. "Seeds of Hope." *The Ecologist,* 1983, *13,* 175–178.

Hochstedler, E. *Corporations as Criminals.* Beverly Hills, Calif.: Sage, 1984.

Hudson, H. *Telecommunications and Development.* Norwood, N.J.: Ablex, 1983.

Hughes, B. B. *World Futures: A Critical Analysis of Alternatives.* Baltimore, Md.: Johns Hopkins University Press, 1985.

Irwin, M. R. "Markets Without Boundaries." *Telecommunications Policy,* 1984, *8,* 12–14.

Jain, S. C. "Environmental Scanning in U.S. Corporations." *Long Range Planning,* 1984, *17,* 117–128.

Jhirad, D. J. *Renewable Energy for Industrialization and Development.* Boulder, Colo.: Westview, 1984.

Jick, T. "What Is Managerial Competency?" Working Paper, York University, Toronto, 1984.

Jorge, A. (ed.). *Trade, Debt and Growth in Latin America.* New York: Pergamon Press, 1984.

Kieffer, J. A. *Gaining the Dividends of Longer Life: New Roles for Older Workers.* Boulder, Colo.: Westview, 1983.

Kirk, M. "The Return of Malthus? The Global Demographic Future, 2000–2050." *Futures,* 1984, *16,* 124–138.

Kwitney, J. *Endless Enemies: The Making of an Unfriendly World.* New York: Congdon & Weed, 1984.

Lewin, K. *Field Theory in Social Science.* New York: Harper & Row, 1951.

Lund, R. T. "Remanufacturing." *Technology Review,* 1984, *87,* 18–29.

Lyons, R. D. "End of Most Tooth Decay Predicted for Near Future." *The New York Times,* Dec. 20, 1983, p. C1.

MacFadyen, J. T. *Gaining Ground: The Renewal of America's Small Farms.* New York: Holt, Rinehart & Winston, 1984.

Machan, T. R., and Johnson, M. B. (eds.). *Rights and Regulation: Ethical, Political, and Economic Issues.* Cambridge, Mass.: Ballinger, 1983.

McKnight, J., and Kretzmann, J. "Community Organizing in the 80s: Toward a Post-Alinsky Agenda." *Social Policy,* 1984, *14,* 15–17.

McNamara, R. S. "Time Bomb or Myth: The Population Problem." *Foreign Affairs,* 1984, *62,* 1107–1131.

McNamara, R. S. "South Africa: The Middle East of the 1990s?" *The New York Times,* Oct. 24, 1984, p. E21.

Makin, J. H. *The Global Debt Crisis: America's Growing Involvement.* New York: Basic Books, 1984.

Malik, R. "Japan's Fifth Generation Computer Project." *Futures,* 1983, *15,* 205–210.

Marien, M. "Some Questions for the Information Society." *World Future Society Bulletin,* 1983, *17,* 17–23.

Marien, M. (ed.). *Future Survey: A Monthly Abstract of Books, Articles, and Reports Concerning Forecasts, Trends, and Ideas About the Future.* Bethesda, Md.: World Future Society, 1983–1986.

Mathisen, T. *A Study of Global Integration.* New York: Columbia University Press, 1984.

Maurice, C., and Smithson, C. W. *The Doomsday Myth: 100,000 Years of Economic Crises.* Stanford, Calif.: Hoover Institution Press, 1984.

Mayer, M. *The Money Bazaars: Understanding the Banking Revolution Around Us.* New York: Dutton, 1984.

Monmaey, T. "Yeast at Work: Biotechnology's Workaholic Does More Than Make Bread Rise." *Science,* 1985, *6,* 30-36.

Morgan, G. *Images of Organization.* Newbury Park, Calif.: Sage, 1986.

Morgan, G., and Ramirez, R. "Action Learning: A Holographic Metaphor for Guiding Social Change." *Human Relations,* 1984, *37,* 1-28.

Morley, D. "An Introduction to Search Conferences." Working Paper, York University, Toronto, 1987.

Morley, D., and Ramirez, R. "Food for the Future of Mexico." Occasional Paper, York University Action Learning Group, Toronto, 1983.

Moyer, R. "The Futility of Forecasting." *Long Range Planning,* 1984, *17,* 65-127.

Naisbitt, J. *Megatrends.* New York: Warner, 1982.

National Resource Council. *Energy Use: The Human Dimension.* New York: Freeman, 1984.

National Resource Council. "Computer-Integrated Manufacturing: Barriers and Opportunities." *National Productivity Review,* Spring 1985, pp. 170-178.

Norgaard, R. B. "Coevolutionary Agricultural Development." *Economic Development and Cultural Change,* 1984, *32,* 525-545.

Ohmae, K. *The Mind of the Strategist.* New York: McGraw-Hill, 1982.

Ohmae, K. *Triad Power: The Coming Shape of Global Competition.* New York: Free Press, 1985.

Otway, H. J., and Peltu, M. (eds.). *New Office Technology: Human and Organizational Aspects.* Norwood, N.J.: Ablex, 1983.

Ouchi, W. *The M Form Society: How American Teamwork Can Capture the Competitive Edge.* Reading, Mass.: Addison-Wesley, 1984.

Peitchinis, S. G. *Computer Technology and Employment.* New York: St. Martin's Press, 1983.

Perpich, J. G. (ed.). "Biotechnology: Impact on Societal Institutions." *Technology in Society,* 1983, *5*(1), 1–49; *5*(2), 83–118.

Peters, T., and Waterman, R., Jr. *In Search of Excellence.* New York: Harper & Row, 1982.

Pollak, R. "Solar Power: The Promise Fades." *The Progressive,* 1984, *48,* 32–35.

Postel, S. *Air Pollution, Acid Rain, and the Future of Forests.* Worldwatch Paper 58. Washington, D.C.: Worldwatch Institute, 1984a.

Postel, S. *Water: Rethinking Management in an Age of Scarcity.* Washington, D.C.: Worldwatch Institute, 1984b.

Prentis, S. *Biotechnology: A New Industrial Revolution.* New York: George Braziller, 1984.

Ramirez, R. "Action Learning: A Strategic Approach for Organizations Facing Turbulent Environments." *Human Relations,* 1983, *36,* 210–215.

Regan, T. *The Case for Animal Rights.* Berkeley: University of California Press, 1983.

Reinhold, R. "Machines Built to Emulate Human Experts' Reasoning." *The New York Times,* Mar. 29, 1984, p. 1.

Revans, R. "Action Learning: A Management Development Program." *Personnel Review,* 1971, *11,* 36–44.

Revans, R. *Action Learning.* Bromley, England: Chartwell Bratt, 1982.

Rodale, R. "Regenerative Technology." *Resurgence,* 1983, *98,* 32–34.

Rogers, P. "The Future of Water." *The Atlantic Monthly,* July 1983, 80–92.

Rosen, C. "Employee Stock Ownership Plans: A New Way to Work." *Business Horizons,* 1983, *26,* 48–54.

Schiller, H. I. *Information and the Crisis Economy.* Norwood, N.J.: Ablex, 1984.

Scrimshaw, N. S. "The Politics of Starvation." *Technology Review,* 1984, *87,* 27–78.

Serrin, W. "After Years of Decline, Sweatshops Are Back." *The New York Times,* Oct. 12, 1983, p. A1.

Shaikh, R. A., and Nichols, J. K. "The International Management of Chemicals." *Ambio: A Journal of the Human Environment,* 1984, *13,* 88–91.

Sheaffer, J. R., and Stevens, L. A. *Future Water: An Exciting*

Solution to America's Most Serious Resource Crisis. New York: William Morrow, 1983.

Snyder, D. P., and Edwards, G. *Future Forces: An Association Executive's Guide to a Decade of Change and Choice.* Washington, D.C.: The Foundation of the American Society of Association Executives, 1984.

Stavrianos, L. S. *The Promise of the Coming Dark Age.* San Francisco: Freeman, 1976.

Stewart, R. *Choices for the Manager.* New York: McGraw–Hill, 1982.

Sylvester, E. J. *The Gene Age: Genetic Engineering and the Next Industrial Revolution.* New York: Scribner's, 1983.

Taylor, A. M. "Canada 2001: Alternative Futures for the Canadian Communities." *World Futures,* 1982, *18,* 177–221.

Thurow, L. "Revitalizing American Industry: Managing in a Competitive World Economy." *California Management Review,* 1984, *27,* 9–41.

Tobias, M. (ed.). *Deep Ecology.* San Diego, Calif.: Avant Books, 1984.

Tolchin, S. J., and Tolchin, M. *Dismantling America: The Rush to Deregulate.* Boston: Houghton Mifflin, 1983.

Trist, E. L. "Action Research and Adaptive Planning." In A. W. Clark (ed.), *Experimenting with Organizational Life.* New York: Plenum, 1976.

Trist, E. L. "The Evolution of Sociotechnical Systems as a Conceptual Framework and as an Action Research Program." In A. H. Van de Ven and W. F. Joyce (eds.), *Perspectives on Organization Design and Behavior.* New York: Wiley, 1982.

U.S. Congress, Office of Technology Assessment. *Commercial Biotechnology: An International Analysis.* Washington, D.C.: U.S. Government Printing Office, 1984a.

U.S. Congress, Office of Technology Assessment. *Computerized Manufacturing Automation: Employment, Education, and the Workplace.* Washington, D.C.: U.S. Government Printing Office, 1984b.

U.S. Congress, Office of Technology Assessment. *Effects of Information Technology on Financial Service Systems.* Washington, D.C.: U.S. Government Printing Office, 1984c.

U.S. Council on Environmental Quality and the Department of

State. *The Global 2000 Report to the President: Entering the Twenty-First Century.* Washington, D.C.: U.S. Government Printing Office, 1980.

Weyrich, P. M., and Marshner, C. (eds.). *Future 21: Directions for America in the 21st Century.* Greenwich, Conn.: Devin-Adair, 1984.

Whyte, W. F., and Boynton, D. (eds.). *Higher-Yielding Human Systems for Agriculture.* Ithaca, N.Y.: Cornell University Press, 1983.

Williams, T. A. *Learning to Manage Our Futures.* New York: Wiley, 1982.

Yoxen, E. *The Gene Business: Who Should Control Biotechnology?* New York: Harper & Row, 1984.

Zagoria, D. S. "China's Quiet Revolution." *Foreign Affairs,* 1984, 879–904.

🎐🎐🎐 Index

A

Accountability: in networks, 130; stakeholder, 129
Ackoff, R. L., 193, 194
Agriculture, chemical-intensive, fracture analysis for, 23-25
Ambiguity: and decentralized management, 90-93; managing, 125-135
Argyris, C., 193, 194
Asia, and global competition, 149
Australia, and global competition, 149

B

Brainstorming, and creativity, 73-76

C

Canada: background on, 152-156; business and society views in, 152-167; competition in, 136-152, 157, 175, 178; context in, 13-14; contextual competencies in, 156-167; discussions in, 1-2; education in, 148-149, 158-160; and globalization, 149-152; government regulation in, 140-142, 162-164; labor-management relations in, 142-143; national influences on, 137-152; political leadership of, 145-146, 161-162; psyche of, 143-145; research project in, 193-200; resource-based economy of, 138, 140; vision in, 146-148; weaknesses in, 139
Change: attitudes toward, 112-113; buying into, 72; and competence programs, 168-184; of competencies and contexts, 136-167; complexity and ambiguity managed for, 125-135; creativity, learning, and innovation for, 69-85; and decentralized management, 86-95; emerging, 1-15; in environment, 16-26; human resources management for, 54-68; and information technologies, 96-124; line-driven, 115-116; packaging, 43-44; and proactive management, 27-45; relishing, 57-61; and security-flexibility dilemma, 59-61; vision for, 46-53
Chemical-intensive agriculture, fracture analysis for, 23-25
Communication: of actionable vision, 48-53; for creativity, 80-82; speeded up, 107-108
Competence: analysis of programs for, 168-184; and appropriateness, 170; contextual, 13-15; C-PLAN for, 170-183, 185-192; of empowering, 17; and implica-

tions for management education, 184; integrated program
for, 178-179; mindset for, 168-
170; need for new, 1-15; research methodology for, 193-
200
Competition: analysis of Canadian
view of, 136-167; background
on, 136-137; and business and
society views, 152-167; in culture, 71-72; national influences
on, 137-152; and outside-in
management, 37-41
Computer literacy, and information
technology, 111-112, 118
Control, and chaos balanced, in creativity, 44-45, 83-85
C-PLAN: and action plans, 178-
179; analysis of, 170-183; background on, 170-171, 174; benefits of, 181-183; concept of, 171;
conditions for, 174; and critical
issues, 177-178; and documentation, 192; and evolutionary design, 191-192; and facilitation,
189-190; focus of, 187-188; and
fracture analysis, 174-177; and
interorganizational forums, 179-
180; mindset for, 185-186; resources for developing, 185-192;
and strategic planning, 180-181;
strategy-driven, 172-173; and
structure, 188-189; synthesis,
framing, and reframing for, 190-
191; variety for, 186-187
Creativity, learning, and innovation: analysis of promoting, 69-
85; and brainstorming, 73-76;
control and chaos balanced in,
83-85; culture for, 70-73, 75-76,
77, 81; discipline balanced with,
44-45; encouraging, 73-83; experimental bias in, 82; and flattened hierarchy, 78-80; and information technology, 81, 97,
99-113; lateral interactions for,
80-82; and pressures, 75-76, 85;
rewards for, 83; shock and surprise for, 78; time out for, 82-
83; and variety, 76-77
Culture: for creativity, learning,
and innovation, 70-73, 75-76,
77, 81; information technology
in, 113; ingredients in, 71-73;
and Just-in-Time management,
22

D

Decentralization: and ambiguity,
90-93; analysis of management
skills for, 86-95; and client-oriented specialist staff, 93-95; and
helicopter management, 86-87;
and self-organization, 89-90; and
umbilical cord management, 88-
89
Decision making, and information
technology, 11, 107-108
Dialogue, and information management, 121

E

Education: in Canada, 148-149;
and human resources management, 67-68; links with, 158-
160; management, 184
Emery, F. E., 194
Emery, M., 193, 194, 195
Empowerment: by C-PLAN, 187-
188; of human resources, 54-68;
from information technology,
107; and leadership, 50; of managers, 17-26; of staff, for decentralized management, 92
Environment: analysis of reading,
16-26; background on, 16-17;
and empowering managers for
future, 17, 20-26; of equals, managing, 65-67; fracture analysis
for, 20-25; and outside-in management, 32-41; paths of opportunity in, 25-26; trends in, 17-
19; turbulence increasing in, 2,
4

Europe, and global competition, 149

Excellence, and management, 132-133

F

Feedback systems, for decentralized management, 91

Flattened hierarchy: and creativity, 78-80; impact of, 8-9; and information technology, 104

Flexibility: and security, 59-61; and small size, 110

Forums: fracture-line, 176-177, 186-187; interorganizational, 179-180, 187

Fracture analysis: for chemical-intensive agriculture, 23-25; and C-PLAN, 174-175, 176-177; for environment, 20-25; and Just-in-Time management, 21-23; and paths of opportunity, 25-26; in research project, 196-197

Fracture-line forums: and competence, 176-177; variety in, 186-187

France, context in, 13-14

H

Helicopter management, and decentralization, 86-87

Hierarchy, flattened, 8-9, 78-80, 140

Hockin, A., 196

Human resources management: analysis of, 54-68; background on, 54-55; change relished in, 57-61; and competence, 183; and education, 67-68; and environment of equals, 65-67; and human and technical aspects, 64-65; importance of, 7-8; people as key in, 55-57; and security-flexibility issue, 59-61; and skills and perspectives broadened, 62-64; specialists and generalists in, 61-65

I

Information technologies: analysis of harnessing, 96-124; and attitudes toward change, 112-113; background on, 96-97; and computer literacy, 111-112, 118; creative use of, 97, 99-113; data and information in, 119-121; and decision making, 11, 107-108; and dialogue, 121; impact of, 9-12, 98; implications of, 99-100, 124; and Just-in-Time system, 10, 100-101, 102-103, 105, 123; overload in, 118-121; and planning, 113-118; and products and services, 97, 99-103; and reductions for efficiency, 106; and restructured systems, 101-102; and small size, 108-110; software strategic to, 12, 122-124; trends in, 97, 99; and work design, 103-107

Innovation. *See* Creativity, learning, and innovation

Interorganizational forums: for competence, 179-180; variety in, 187

J

Japan: competition in, 122; context in, 13-14; and global competition, 149, 175-176

Just-in-Time (JIT) management: culture of, 22; and fracture analysis, 21-23; and information technology, 10, 100-101, 102-103, 105, 123; and networks of stakeholders, 129

K

Korea, and global competition, 149-150

L

Lateral interactions, for creativity, 80-82

Lateral thinking, and creativity, 74
Leadership: broad process of, 50-53; and empowerment, 50; as framing or bridging, 6; importance of, 6-7; and proactive mindset, 31-32; and symbols, 49-50; values, direction, and responsibility in, 53
Learning. *See* Creativity, learning, and innovation
Lewin, K., 193

M

Management: background on, 125-126; complexity of, 12-13; of complexity and ambiguity, 125-135; and education links, 158-160; either-or thinking in, 133; entrepreneurial and creative aspects of, 65; in environment of equals, 65-67; and excellence, 132-133; future scenarios for, 2-15; helicopter, 86-87; of human resources, 54-68; of multiple meanings, 133-134; of multiple stakeholders, 126-132; of networks, 129-130; outside-in, 5, 32-41; proactive, 27-45; remote, 86-95; simultaneous, 132-134; of transition, 134-135; umbilical cord, 88-89
Management information systems (MIS): client orientation of, 93-95; and line-driven change, 115-116
Managers: bridge building by, 156-161; collaboration by, 14; competence programs for, 168-184; contextual competencies of, 156-167; education for, 184; empowering, for future, 17, 20-26; facilitation skills of, 189-190; and government expenditures, 161-162; human and technical aspects for, 64-65; national and local actions by, 164-165; and partnerships, 160-161; proactive, 4-6; reframing by, 161-164; and

regulations, 162-164; skills needed by, 66-67, 168-169, 189-190; social responsibility of, 14-15, 165-167; as specialists and generalists, 61-65
Market: customer view of, 34; and outside-in management, 33-35
Menzel, B., 196
Mindset: for competence, 168-170; for C-PLAN, 185-186; proactive, 4-5, 27-32
Morgan, G., 193, 194, 196, 197
Morley, D., 194, 195

N

Networks, organizations in, 129-130

O

Optimism, in culture, 72
Organization: in networks, 129-130; stakeholder concept of, 126-129
Outside-in management: and competition, 37-41; concept of, 5; and frontiers for development, 35-39; and market, 33-35; as proactive, 32-41

P

Partnerships, and value differences, 160-161
Peterson, R., 196
Planning: bottom-up, 116; for competence, 170-183, 185-192; consistency in, 116-117; evolutionary, 113-118; and information technology, 11-12; integration issue in, 114-115, 116-117; and line-driven change, 115-116; and stakeholders, 128-129; strategic, 180-181; and training, 118; user involvement in, 117-118
Positioning and repositioning: balancing creativity and discipline for, 44-45; concept of, 5-6; pack-

aging change for, 43-44; and risk-taking, 41-43; skills for, 41-45; timing important in, 45
Proactive management: developing mindsets for, 27-32; from outside in, 32-41; positioning and repositioning skills for, 41-45
Proactive mindsets: concept of, 4-5; developing, 27-32; forward mode for, 28-29; and leadership, 31-32; and opportunity seeking, 29-30; and positives from negatives, 30-31
Putnam, R., 193

R

Ramirez, R., 193, 194, 197
Research project: action-learning approach to, 194; analysis of, 193-200; discussion groups for, 198-200; inquiry process in, 197-200; methodology for, 196-197; requirements of, 195-196; results of, 199-200
Revans, R., 193, 194

S

Scandinavia: context in, 13-14; self-regulation in, 163
Schön, D., 194
Self-organization, and decentralization, 89-90
Self-questioning, culture for, 72-73
Shell Canada, and research project, 193, 196
Smith, D. M., 193
Software industry, and information technology, 12, 122-124
Stakeholders: accountability of, 129; multiple, management of, 126-132; and networks, 129-130; and organization, 126-129; and planning, 128-129; potpourri of, 130-132; recognizing, 128; and remote management, 131
Sweden, self-regulation in, 163

Systems design, conditions for, 116-117

T

Taylor, B., 196
Tebb, W., 196
Technology. *See* Information technologies
Time out, for creativity, 82-83
Timing, in positioning and repositioning, 45
Training, and planning, 118
Trist, E. L., 193, 194

U

Umbilical cord management, and decentralization, 88-89
United Kingdom, context in, 13-14
United States: competition with, 136, 138, 141, 149, 151, 162, 176; context in, 13-14

V

Values: adding, 72; and leadership, 53; in partnerships, 160-161; regulation through, 162-164; shared, and creativity, 84-85
Variety, requisite, 77, 186
Vision: actionable, 48-53; analysis of sharing, 46-53; in Canada, 146-148; as frame for action, 47-48; and leadership, 49-53

W

Wade, D., 196
Williams, T. A., 194
Women, managerial qualities in, 8, 67
Work design, and information technology, 103-107

Y

York University, and research project, 193, 196